Rays of Light

Rays of Light

Ginninderra Press – the first 20 years

Edited by Joan Fenney

Rays of Light: Ginninderra Press – the first 20 years
ISBN 978 1 76041 143 5
Copyright © text Joan Fenney and individual contributors 2016
Cover photo: Chris Matthews

First published 2016 by
GINNINDERRA PRESS
PO Box 3461 Port Adelaide 5015
www.ginninderrapress.com.au

Contents

Ginninderra Press – The First 20 Years	Joan Fenney	7
Stones Across a River	Thérèse Corfiatis	46
Stepping Stones	Bill Cotter	52
From the Darkness to the Light	Brenda Eldridge	57
Finding a Voice	Ian McFarlane	65
Sincerely Speaking	Maureen Mitson	73
Silk Road	Ann Nadge	81
Alive the Spirit	Barbara Olds	84
Finding the Light	Zenda Vecchio	88
Awards & Commendations		94
About the Contributors		97
Acknowledgements		99
Afterword	Stephen Matthews	101

Ginninderra Press – The First 20 Years

Joan Fenney

> To be a part of something that allows somebody's voice to be transferred to the written page, and to share in the author's excitement, is huge. I've been determined to keep the press going since its inception in 1996... I'll continue doing this, because I must do it.

From first light, thousands of words stream into the Port Adelaide office of Ginninderra Press every day. Publishers Stephen Matthews and Brenda Eldridge are surrounded by manuscripts amid the vast number of books around the walls of their light-filled home nestled by the tidal reach. Dolphins glide and leap through the air as they journey along the Port River in full view of the floor-to-ceiling windows of the rented town house where Stephen and Brenda live and work. A kaleidoscope of birds from honeyeaters to parrots fly around the native-plant haven Stephen and Brenda have created in their front and rear gardens. Seasonal vegetables and scented roses complement the serene setting.

The nature that surrounds Stephen and Brenda is in stark contrast to the whirring of machines that are the pulse of the award-winning Ginninderra Press (GP). Make no mistake, the couple who are lovers of birds, wildlife, plants, the river and sea, have an office featuring the latest technology – computers, printers, iPads, iPhones – needed to operate one of Australia's most successful and enduring independent publishing houses. In an age when book publishing throughout the world is concentrated in the hands of a few multinational conglomerates, independent publishers are rare. Twenty years since its humble beginnings in a spare bedroom of Stephen Matthews's Canberra home, GP is thriving.

> The date that Stephen Matthews brought Ginninderra Press from Canberra to Adelaide should be celebrated yearly. His and Brenda's professionalism and compassion are greatly appreciated. Happy birthday GP!
> *Jude Aquilina*

To explain why GP has survived, when many with good intentions have fallen, is to explore the private but determined life of Stephen, GP's originator.

First words

Words have woven themselves through Stephen's life from a young age. As a shy and quiet boy growing up on a council estate in the small town of Chichester, in England's West Sussex – with three older siblings, a mother lovingly called 'Tiny' and a father working as a post office clerk – Stephen's days were steeped in the written word. Although there were surprisingly few books in his parents' home, Stephen's bedroom was lined with books.

> My parents were not particularly bookish and I rarely went to bookshops with them. However, they liked the fact that I read and were keen to foster this. There was nothing I'd rather do on Saturday mornings than go to the local bookshop. I must have liked the peacefulness of the shop – full of Penguin and Pelican books. It was a solitary act, not something I shared with anyone else. I liked reading adventure books, especially those by the English author Arthur Catherall, and Enid Blyton's Famous Five. At secondary school I read a lot of ancient history, as it was connected to my studies in Greek and Latin, and for enjoyment I read Perry Mason.[1]

Writing was never Stephen's true passion but books and the ideas they generated fuelled his imagination and increased his knowledge. However, it was in his high school years that his first publishing foray took shape and no doubt a seed was planted with this endeavour that would stay at the back of his mind ready to develop in the future.

> A friend and I were interested in cars and we started a club that was boringly called the Auto Club and we produced a little magazine. It was usually four sides of foolscap paper. We wrote all the copy and then gave it to my friend's mother, who was a typist, and she typed it up on one of those old Roneo stencils. We sold it to all our friends for threepence a copy. We kept producing it for three to four years until our ways parted towards the end of high school.

It is evident to anyone who spends time with Stephen that, although he is very modest and humble, he is a wordsmith who is fiercely intelligent. Such was his ability that he excelled at high school and headed to the prestigious Cambridge University

---

I consider myself fortunate that Ginninderra Press published my poetry. I recommend Stephen for his thoughtful and intelligent approach to publication and his great attention to detail.
Elaine Barker

in 1965 to study Classics. He didn't enjoy university and found the approach to the teaching of Classics dry and sterile. He quickly swapped to the interestingly named Moral Science course, which encompassed areas of philosophy.

Stephen wanted to be involved with student newspapers at Cambridge but he said they were a closed shop. 'You had to know someone working on the papers and I was easily discouraged. I was still very shy and lacking in confidence.'

On completing his degree, Stephen contemplated the idea of pursuing a career in publishing – as he 'read a lot and was fascinated by the way books were constructed'. However, he was stopped in his tracks by a university careers counsellor.

> He told me there would be no vacancies in publishing for someone like me. I really don't know why he said that but I guess it was because I didn't have the right social connections, and as a naive 21-year-old I didn't challenge his assertion. Instead, he advised me that I would be better suited to a career in teaching.

To Stephen's later regret, he acted on the counsellor's advice. In 1969, following the completion of a year's postgraduate teaching course, Stephen found himself in Bideford, in rural North Devon, at a 300-pupil school, teaching primary school-age children from the equivalent of Australian Years Three to Seven. He stayed there for four years before accepting the headmastership of a two-teacher school in West Down, also in North Devon.

Unfortunately, Stephen found teaching not to be the fulfilling career he yearned for.

> For a while I was driven by it, I suppose, and as a result was given my first headship at 28. There weren't many 28-year-old headmasters at that stage and I was ambitious until then. It wasn't so much the teaching, or the interaction with children – it was the parents particularly in a small cut-off little English village that turned me off teaching as they were very small-minded. By about 1977 I was already looking for ways to escape from teaching, either by finding an educational administration job or starting a bookshop. My first wife and I spent quite a lot of time looking at bookshops that were for sale but there was no way we could have afforded to pursue that venture.

Changing chapters

After five years at West Down, a marriage break-up saw Stephen arrive in Australia in

---

In accepting my Shards of Ice, Stephen recognised and acknowledged a voice which others feared or dared not print. Thanks to his vision, now it is out there and appreciated.
Minnie Biggs

1979 with his son, then nearly eight years old. Although Stephen knew very little about Australia, friends he had taught with in the UK had made the move and recommended this distant country to him. Initially, Stephen joined his English friends in the Northern Territory, where he spent a year teaching at a one-teacher primary school in Daly River before heading to Adelaide. After stints working as a bookseller to school librarians, and as a project officer for the Catholic Education Office based in the Riverland, Stephen then headed to Canberra to work as a teacher/librarian in a private school. However, he was looking to find a career that he could be passionate about.

> I finally escaped teaching in 1986 and early the following year a very sensible person in the Co-op bookshop at the Australian National University gave me a job, and when he left three years later, I was made manager. Although its principal purpose was to sell textbooks it was also a really good general bookshop, selling the quality books I liked to read. At that stage it had a huge turnover of more than a million dollars a year. After a further busy three years at the bookshop, and a stint at Dymocks in Sydney, I spent a year back in Canberra 'resting', as actors would say. During that time I reviewed books and wrote author profiles for *The Canberra Times* and *Australian Book Review*.

In mid-1995, at the end of his 'rest' year, Stephen began working at Green Words, a Canberra-based business specialising in editing and designing company and government reports. He was initially employed as a part-time office manager but when the business owner realised that Stephen possessed extensive English skills, his role increased. He was assigned an editing role as well as managing the office. It was while working at Green Words that Stephen realised that there were a number of people who were bringing in private manuscripts seeking editorial advice, or hoping to get them published.

> As Green Words wasn't in a position to do this, I realised there was a market for a small publishing company in Canberra. The crucial spark for me involved a client who had what in hindsight could have been a terrific book about the way that a corporation in the Riverina had taken over the local cooperative fruit processing plant, and how they had completely ruined it. However, because Green Words wasn't itself a publisher, they would charge clients a fee to do the design, layout and editing. I thought here was a book that really deserved proper publication but it was a shame that somebody had to pay out lots and lots of money and still be thwarted from having a really good end product. It could have been a much better book if the manuscript had been treated better. I wanted to be able to publish manuscripts that would otherwise never see the light of day.

Being published by Ginninderra Press was a wonderful experience.
Brenda and Stephen were professional, patient and efficient throughout.
I feel honoured to be part of the Ginninderra Press family.
J V Birch

New words

So, in July 1996, Ginninderra Press began simply – operating from a small bedroom in Stephen's home in Canberra. He started with the bare basics – a computer, a laser printer and a primitive scanner. A friend who worked at one of the universities gave him a copy of the relevant software that he needed, but could not afford. Stephen is still amazed at how simply GP began.

> It was foolhardy, really. I didn't have a clue about exactly what publishing would involve. It was a reckless thing to do because I had no business plan and no idea if there were enough people who would want to take advantage of what I was going to be doing. It just seemed to me there was room for a small publisher in Canberra. My intention was to do report editing, and to use the limited technology I had to produce modest forms of print on demand publications from a home office.

Finally, 28 years after the university careers counsellor had steered Stephen away from the career he wanted to pursue, he had taken the first step to realising his publishing dream. It is not hard to detect in the years leading up to the birth of GP that there was a restlessness in Stephen, moving from teaching to bookselling, back to teaching, book reviewing and then doing editing, layout work and office administration.

> I was fumbling my way along, escaping from one job to another – it was all part of my uncertainty, in both my professional and personal life.

However, it is evident that all of the jobs that Stephen had undertaken before he founded GP contributed to the skills and experience he needed to start his own publishing house. His knowledge of bookselling, editing, layout work, writing, book reviewing and interviewing authors, not to mention his being an avid reader of a wide variety of literature, combined to provide the knowledge he needed for a career in publishing. Not to forget that his years of teaching and dealing with children, school administrators and, as he would say, some 'difficult' parents' have proven vital in giving Stephen the patience he requires to work with challenging authors.

Also, Stephen possessed that vital trait – determination – which meant that he was able to rise above obstacles and operate on a shoestring to follow his dream and become a publisher. No doubt the elitist words of the careers counsellor would have been at the back of this very proud man's mind.

> For a pencil and paper poet, the path to publication is arduous.
> Stephen and Brenda gave the extra help needed, Brenda
> boosting my confidence by sending handwritten cards.
> *Avril Bradley*

One of the earliest choices Stephen faced in starting the business was to decide on the very important name he would give the press. As he lived at the time in a town house development called Silver Gums, Stephen eagerly embraced the idea of naming his publishing venture Silver Gums Press. However, he concedes, he didn't do his research properly and there was already a Melbourne-based publishing house operating under the name Silver Gum Press, and fairly quickly they foreshadowed legal action should he continue with his chosen name. However, as some of the best decisions and discoveries are made when relaxing, Stephen, like Archimedes, hit upon his light-bulb moment for a new name for his publishing house while in the bathtub.

> I was thinking about how Canberra publishers like Brindabella Press had chosen a local name and I thought here we are near Lake Ginninderra, Ginninderra Falls and Ginninderra Drive – so it was logical to name Ginninderra Press due to its location. I thought nobody interstate would choose that name. A couple of years later when I was looking in a book about Canberra place names, I discovered that 'ginninderra' is an Aboriginal word meaning 'throwing out little rays of light'. How apt!

There is no evidence to suggest that after Stephen's Eureka moment he followed the rumoured lead of the Greek scholar and raced along the streets of Canberra *sans* clothes!

Stephen admits to having no detailed vision for what he hoped to achieve with GP but he knew he wanted to guide people through the publishing process. Firstly, he was keen to assist people who were being charged too much for having their work edited and laid out. He knew he could do this at a much cheaper rate. Secondly, Stephen wanted to help people publish their shorter works with the benefit of his publishing skills.

After some initial publicity in the local press, manuscripts started arriving from local authors, and word spread so quickly that submissions were soon arriving from all over Australia. The challenge Stephen faced was deciding which publishing model he should follow. Initially, GP books were stapled in A5 size and limited to 64 pages – a format that was best suited to collections of poetry and short stories. Non-fiction was published in A4-sized books with comb binding. According to Stephen, the buyers of these publications were interested in their content rather than wanting beautifully bound books.

A once in a life time experience for me, publishing my poems, and I was given total commitment and efficiency, as well as personal attention, by Ginninderra Press.
Helene Castles

Soon, writers began bringing in longer manuscripts, which could not be produced in either of these formats.

> I think the first person who brought me a longer manuscript actually suggested the model that we followed for quite a few years – where the author would pay for the cost of printing in return for repayments over the course of sales. Unfortunately, that's where a lot of misapprehension about the way we operated came from, and GP was being labelled in some quarters as a vanity press. No matter how many times I said, 'No, the writers are not paying me, they're paying the printer and they'll get their money back if they sell their book,' that explanation wasn't understood by a lot of people.

From the beginning GP paid royalties of 12½ per cent to authors, which was above the standard rate of 10 per cent. Stephen believed there had to be some small compensation for the fact that 'due to being published by a small, independent press, people weren't going to become rich and weren't going to be selling heaps of books'. Also, if authors bought copies of their books to sell, they received an author discount of 40 or 45 per cent, depending on the number of copies they bought.

Another publishing model Stephen introduced in 1999 was thermal-bound books that did not require authors to pay for the printing. This was GP's early attempt at print on demand books and allowed more pages than the original stapled books. Stephen produced these books in-house and it meant they could be printed in whatever number, large or small, the author required. The authors still received royalties and could also purchase the books at the author discount of 40 or 45 per cent.

The most significant difference that separates GP from being classified as a vanity press is that from GP's earliest days, Stephen chose which books he wanted to publish. He has clearly stated that 'no one can buy me!' From the hundreds of manuscripts he was receiving, he only chose to publish about 10 per cent of them. He has always stressed he wants to publish books that 'touch me – both on an emotional and intellectual level. The author needs to show they have something to impart, that they have the ability to shine a light in dark corners, and be able to share that with the reader.'

In fact, following the trial publication of the 1996 collection of Stephen's interviews for *The Canberra Times* titled *Stirring the Imagination* Volume 1, one of the first books Stephen accepted for publication and the first GP book to have a launch

---

I feel that having two collections of poetry published by Ginninderra Press validates my worth as a poet.
Jennifer Chrystie

was *Homesick* – a collection of poems and stories about domestic violence.

> The collection was written by two friends, one from Bega, NSW, and the other from Canberra, and both had been in abusive relationships. The stories were fiction but resulted from their own experiences. I published it because I have always wanted to publish books that have some social importance, an edge of social consciousness, which reflects GP's connection to 'rays of light'. Domestic abuse wasn't discussed much in 1996, so it was, and still is, a significant subject that needed light shed on it.

The early days of GP were financially tough for Stephen but he never once questioned his decision to start the press, or regretted venturing into his long-awaited foray into the publishing world.

> I loved it from the start. I never wanted to stop. My wife at the time famously asked me after a year or two if we were rich yet. I had to explain to her that we probably were never going to be. Often there wasn't enough money to buy a ream of paper in order to print the books. My friend at the university somehow managed to find paper to tide me over. But it never occurred to me to stop. Why would I have wanted to stop when finally I had reconnected myself to what I wanted to do back when I left university? I was now responsible for my own choices and decisions, so I never had any doubt that I would keep pursuing my publishing dream.

Stephen may stress that he had no clear vision when he started GP but he was certainly adamant from the start about the genres he wanted to publish. The non-fiction he wanted to publish covered the subjects he was interested in – history, education, sociology and social issues. With fiction, he was always and still is looking for stories that have some kind of social edge to them.

> When I publish a book, I want the reader to have learnt something – about themselves,

Many people talk about writing their memoir, or possibly a novel when they retire, but it stays in an old notebook. Ginninderra Press made it happen for me.
Ray Clift

about the author, about history, or about modern life. I want the reader to be changed at the end in some way, however limited that may be.

However, one of the genres GP publishes most – poetry – was not something that Stephen thought would occupy such a large proportion of his publications. It was not until he started receiving manuscripts that he realised how many people write poetry and that there were so few publishing options available. The early years of GP coincided with a retreat by large publishing houses from producing poetry and short stories due to limited sales and the rise of marketing departments which find it easier to publicise 'name' authors. However, Stephen quickly added both genres to GP's publication list.

> Publishing poetry fits into the same kind of focus as fiction and non-fiction that I'm interested in, because writing poetry helps poets understand the world we live in. If their message is conveyed, other people can gain from the poet's insight. The same applies to the short story collections I publish. In many ways, short story writers are like poetry writers – they're both involved in this great act of distillation and compression.

GP's second year of operation saw Stephen being recognised for his work and he was thrilled to win the Canberra Critics Circle Award for Literature for his 'tireless contribution to the writing community', in October 1997. The following year, as well as continuing to establish the press, Stephen managed to find time to edit *Eye of the Soul*, a collection published by *Magpies Magazine* of interviews he had conducted with writers for children and young adults.

Offshoots

Three years after GP started, it quickly became a place of ideas due to Stephen's openness to new ventures and his willingness to keep the press evolving and moving with the times (which is clearly evident in recent times with the expansion of publishing into the digital age). Early in 1999, established Canberra poets Geoff Page and Alan Gould approached Stephen to see if he would be interested in having a high-class poetry imprint operating under the banner of GP. They recognised the publishing skills and reputation Stephen had gained and when he readily agreed, Indigo was born.

Geoff and Alan had total creative control to select manuscripts from poets to be

---

An equally visionary and welcoming publishing house that has contributed significantly to the enduring state and quality of literature in this country over the past twenty years.
Robbie Coburn

published in quality-designed books under the Indigo banner. Twenty-three titles were produced from 1999 to 2011 – featuring work by individual poets, and anthologies including *The Indigo Book of Modern Australian Sonnets* edited by Geoff Page and *The Indigo Book of Australian Prose Poems* edited by Michael Byrne.

Later in 1999, short story author Craig Cormick approached Stephen about starting Mockingbird, another imprint of GP, which would publish short stories. Twenty-eight books were published until 2011, including a number of collections written by Craig, one of which, *A Funny Thing Happened at 27,000 Feet*, won the Arts Queensland Steele Rudd Australian Short Story Award in 2006. (See page 94 for a list of GP's other award-winning books.)

At this time, poets and short story writers, both newcomers and those established ones with a lengthy track record, were discovering that outlets for their work were difficult to find.

Spreading the word

From GP's earliest days, Stephen was thinking of ways to promote his authors and their books. He was mindful that as a small publishing house he was not able to provide a full-scale distribution system due to a lack of funds to employ full-

Jacaranda Song, a Pocket Poet, my first with Ginninderra Press, really sang to me. I was encouraged to publish *Pour a Libation* with such helpful, patient people at the helm.
Dawn Colsey

time sales representatives who could visit bookshops around the country promoting GP books. Also, additional copies of books would need to be printed to provide trial copies to distributors, which was not possible for a one-man operation due to the costs and administration required.

Hence, author launches became a crucial vehicle to maximise sales and ensure GP's survival – often amounting to a quarter or even a half of a book's total sales. Launches were initially held in Canberra but it wasn't long before launches were being held in Sydney, Melbourne, Adelaide and Hobart, as well as in regional centres. Stephen developed this idea further and began to hold highly innovative GP events which involved launching two or three books at the event, as well as panel discussions where a wide variety of topics were discussed by authors, ranging from Writing from the Dark and Fighting the Black Dog through to Are You Brave Enough to be a Poet?

The events, which were and still are free for participants, provided the opportunity for GP to gain publicity in *The Canberra Times* and local newspapers, and their support was vital to the success of these well-received events for readers and writers. As well as promoting the events, *The Canberra Times* sometimes profiled the authors that were featured. Also, importantly, the events and launches created concentrated selling opportunities for GP books.

The introduction of annual GP short story competitions was another vital way the press was promoted to writers and writers' groups around the country. The competitions were held for six years beginning in 2000. They proved extremely popular and at their peak 250 entries were being received. Alongside this model, an additional short story competition was held for children's writers that ran from 2002 to 2006. Stephen acknowledges that the books that comprised the stories judged as the best each year did not sell many copies. However, he noted, 'The publicity we received promoting the competition, and the publication of the books, were vital to giving GP a strong presence.'

A new voice

As part of Stephen's willingness and eagerness to be open to ideas from the public, he was approached by local Canberra identity and former staffer at the National Library, Bill Tully, and novelist, essayist, poet and reviewer, Ian McFarlane, of Bermagui, NSW, with the idea of producing a magazine whose contributors would comment

---

> To have been published by Ginninderra Press over the years has been of great joy to me and I thank them for the opportunity to exhibit my writing.
> Nance Cookson.

on issues of the day – especially, as Stephen would say, on 'broad cultural issues, like cultural politics and history'.

After some months of discussions, Stephen agreed to publish *Voice* and joined Bill and Ian on the editorial board. The small quarterly magazine of opinion and review, open to voices that would not normally have access to public expression, was launched in 2002 with a print run of 200 copies. Without a generous benefactor or a government grant, *Voice* was able to exist for 11 years. It was sold mainly through subscriptions and was available at some Canberra bookshops, with a cover price of

The Bega District News 12 March 2004

Rediscovering democracy at grassroots level

A PUBLIC forum in Bermagui on Sunday, March 28, will discuss issues of regional sustainability in an increasingly complex and crowded world.

The forum will be hosted by the Canberra-based magazine, Voice.

"Climate change and global terrorism suggest the 21st century will hold the key to our survival as a human species, and the decisions we take regionally will help make or break our future globally," one of the organisers, Mr Ian McFarlane, said.

"Whatever happens to the world from this point on, it is irrevocably a question of everyone and everything (particularly our survival) being linked.

"For better or worse, we are all involved, which is where the grassroots participation of a democracy driven from the bottom up rather than the top down becomes vitally important.

In March 2002, before a pot-pourri of politicians, poets and passers-by, an independent quarterly of comment and review, Voice, was launched by the editor of The Canberra Times, Mr Jack Waterford.

With the stated intention of democratising social, literary and political comment by helping to facilitate an exchange of ideas from all sources, particularly those outside the established hierarchy, Voice is edited by Mr Bill Tully and Mr Stephen Matthews in Canberra, and local writer and reviewer, Mr Ian McFarlane, who lives at Beauty Point.

Mr McFarlane said the editors took pride in the magazine's unique practice of hosting a public forum to coincide with each issue and reflect the nature of the theme.

In the past, these have included reconciliation, Australian literature, asylum seekers and globalisation.

To celebrate the start of its third year, Voice is holding a public forum on regional sustainability ("The Good, the Green and the Greedy") in the Bermagui Community Hall between 2pm and 4pm on Sunday, March 28.

The forum speakers will be Maggi Hughes, manager of community and cultural services with the Bega Valley Shire Council; Dean Turner from the Crossing Land Education Centre; and Christopher Irons, a PhD scholar and consultant researcher in environmental planning and management.

Entry is free; questions and discussion invited; and refreshments will be served.

The forum is sponsored by the Elm Grove Sanctuary Trust as part of a Ginninderra Press books and writers' day, commencing at 11am.

The program will be as follows: 11am - a poetry reading by Geoff Neville of Bega. 11.30am - a short story reading by Janice Gray of Tura Beach. 11.45am - the launch of 'It's Not Too Late', a collection of stories by Nance Cookson of Millingandi. 12.30pm - a poetry reading by Venie Holmgren of Pambula. 12.45pm - the launch of 'Into the No Zone', a collection of poems by Tim Metcalf of Brogo. 1.15 pm - a poetry reading by Ian McFarlane of Beauty Point. 2pm - the Voice public forum on regional sustainability, 'The Good, the Green and the Greedy'.

For more information phone Ian McFarlane on 6493 4394 or Stephen Matthews on 6258 9060.

•Maggi Hughes, manager of community and cultural services with the Bega Valley Shire Council, will be a speaker at the forum.

Ginninderra Press makes publishing slim volumes by unknown writers possible. Through ebooks I am given a world stage. I am always treated with affection, respect and the best professional standards.
Michele Fermanis-Winward

$5. Every issue had a broad theme and some of these included the environment, indigenous affairs, refugees, and other significant social justice issues.

A significant part of *Voice*'s existence was its instigation of public forums that explored issues raised in the magazine. Some of the topics discussed at the forums included reconciliation, Australian literature, asylum seekers and globalisation. Ian McFarlane noted in an article in *The Canberra Times* at the time that 'One of the things I am most proud of is the public forums. They are grass roots democracy in action. Through the forums, we see ourselves trying to open up the opportunities for debate and discussion.'[2] Stephen added that the key to the success of the forums was their engagement with the community.[3]

Voice ceased publication in 2012 after 11 successful years; like a lot of creative ideas, the energy needed to produce such a magazine had diminished. As Stephen noted,

> It's not that there wasn't the need for people to participate in such an endeavour but that the same group of people ran out of steam. Also, in its own small way, it was caught up in the decline of print magazines.

Sharing stories

It is evident that Stephen created GP as a grassroots publishing house. From the start, GP became part of the Canberra community and then part of the wider Australian community – but always a press for the people, with books written by people from all walks of life, not just a privileged few. Like all effective political candidates who stage the most successful campaigns and win seemingly unwinnable seats, such as Maxine McKew in former Prime Minister John Howard's seat of Bennelong, those who undertake extensive grassroots campaigns get out amongst the community and engage with people and are not afraid of hard work. However, such are the demands of political life that, once they have successfully gained their position, some politicians become removed from everyday life.

This has not been the case with Stephen and Ginninderra Press. Stephen has always sought to interact with the wider community by hosting the before-mentioned free events and launches. Also, he has published books by authors whose work would never have reached the top of mainstream publishers' notorious slush pile – authors who told stories about their families or their experiences in life and may have sold

---

When Stephen published my first poetry book, *Eucalypts and Iris Streams*, in 2002, I had no idea that the next 14 years would see the success of 23 more GP books.
Amelia Fielden

anywhere from 20 to 200 copies. Stories that may have been considered simple and domestic by mainstream publishers as they portray the lives of so-called 'everyday Australians' are in reality unique and extraordinary and resonate with many readers.

GP has published a diverse range of non-fiction books from the amusing and illuminating, to the heartbreaking and thought-provoking stories of human survival – many from first-time authors who are keen to tell their stories. The books have focused on everything from the history of people and places that contribute to our understanding of Australia's local history; colourful characters who epitomise the spirit of Australia's diversity, including the story of one of Australia's authentic torch singers; Houdini's tour of Australia; stories about the trauma of refugees and migrants arriving in Australia; those exploring issues such as negative body image, bullying and poor self-esteem among children; the inspiring story of the front-line contribution of women to the Australian war effort in 1914–1918; tales of dementia; sexual abuse; autism; political memoirs and hundreds more. Stephen is emphatic in his belief for a press that provides opportunities for everyone.

> I believe that all people not just a privileged few have a right to participate actively in cultural production rather than just being passive consumers of mass media. Our culture is enriched when everyone is encouraged to fulfil their creative potential and diminished when that creative potential is stifled or thwarted.

How Did The Fire Know We Lived Here?

The most obvious example of the notion of GP being firmly entrenched as a part of the community was the publishing of the book edited by Stephen that documented the personal stories of people caught up in the devastation of the 2003 Canberra firestorms, *How Did The Fire Know We Lived Here?* This publication, he would add, is one of the highlights of his 20 years in publishing. He saw first-hand the devastation caused by the 18 January firestorms that killed four people, injured more than 490, and destroyed over 500 homes as it tore through in excess of 12 suburbs of Canberra. Suburbs, he has said many times, where barely a tree existed, but such was the power of the firestorms that suburbs were razed flat. Like all Canberrans, especially those people who lost family members, their homes and all their possessions, Stephen was left reeling in the aftermath of such an unexpected catastrophic event.

> My Indian poems in print, to share, has gladdened my heart. GP's professionalism and integrity has made publishing an exciting experience. It's buoyed my self-confidence and stirred my inspiration.
> *Jen Gibson*

Stephen decided to help in the best way he could by documenting this event by inviting residents and firefighters to write personal accounts of their own experiences focusing on the week leading up to the firestorm, the actual day of the fire and the aftermath. More than 100 people shared their stories, poems and photographs in a beautifully-produced 192-page book – featuring tales ranging from poignant to humorous: of a baby born on the day of the fires; the firefighter who feared one of his mates had died; and the man who was relieved that the pile of ironing he had to do went up in flames.

Due to Stephen being so heavily involved in the wider community, he was able to organise local firm Pirion Printers to undertake the printing of the book for free. Stephen donated his time and skill to elicit the stories, design and produce the book. Also, he had the support of *The Canberra Times*, local newspapers and the ABC to help facilitate the gathering of the contributions, and they also helped publicise the finished book. They all combined to enable the stories of the people involved reach a wider audience, as well as helping all those caught up in the fires the chance to start the healing process.

> Being published by Ginninderra Press, firstly as the Hills Poets group and later my own work, gave me confidence and pride.
> *Jill Gower*

Community book raises $73,300 for firestorm appeal

By DANIELLE CRONIN

More than 100 people — who shared their experiences and voiced the community's sentiments in the wake of the January 18 firestorm — helped the healing process yesterday.

In a break between the showers or rain, Chief Minister Jon Stanhope accepted a $73,300 donation for the Bushfire Appeal from the sale of the book — *How Did the Fire Know We Lived Here?*

Four-year-old Hazel Bennett asked her mother that question after bushfires tore through the ACT suburbs, claiming four lives and razing more than 500 homes.

Chauvel Circle, Chapman, was one of the hardest hit streets and about 100 people gathered for the cheque presentation yesterday at No 30, where a driveway and agapanthus remind passers-by that a home once stood on the block.

"This book did something that no individual can achieve," Mr Stanhope said.

"It gave a voice to a community and allows many people affected by the fires to describe in their own words what they experienced and how they felt.

"The response to the book has been overwhelming. The large sales will contribute to easing the pain many hundreds of Canberrans are still feeling as a result of losing their homes and community in the firestorm."

Publisher Ginninderra Press, printer Pirion Pty Ltd and their suppliers donated their time, materials and services to produce the book, which includes stories, poems and photographs from more than 100 contributors.

Stephen Matthews — who put the book together — said the first 3865 copies sold out within two weeks after the April 29 launch.

Yesterday Mr Stanhope launched the second edition, and proceeds from the sale of 3000 copies will help recoup costs incurred during publication of the first edition.

The $73,300 donation brought the Bushfire Appeal total to almost $8.8 million.

"Since the fire hit Canberra, we have achieved a great deal in our endeavours to rebuild and regenerate our community," Mr Stanhope said. "As individuals, and as a community, we have changed as a consequence of January 18 bushfires. I believe we have emerged much wiser and much stronger."

At yesterday's relaunch of the firestorm book, Richard Gibson, Ian O'Connor and Jon Stanhope.

The first print run of the book of 3,500 copies – the largest in the seven-year history of GP to date – sold out in two weeks and raised $73,300 for the Canberra Bushfire Recovery Appeal. Every cent raised was donated to the recovery appeal; no one who took part in printing and publishing the book received any money.

When launching *How Did The Fire Know We Lived Here?* – derived from a four-year-old girl's poignant question after her home was destroyed – ACT Chief Minister at the time, Jon Stanhope, said,

> The book gave voice to the community and allowed people affected to tell their stories. These stories told of the terror, anger, sorrow, love, compassion, humour and hope for the future.[4]

A second print run of just over 3,000 copies also sold quickly and the book has remained the highest-selling GP title to date.

The year was to culminate in Stephen being awarded a Centenary Medal from the Prime Minister's Department for 'his contribution to the writing community and his on-going support for local authors'.

Celebrating 10 years

GP's 10th birthday was a time of great celebration for Stephen – with a mix of pride that he was able to sustain the press for all those years and sheer joy that he had a stable of authors who were seeing their work in print – many for the first time. In the

---

> Ginninderra Press enabled me to dip my poetic toe into publishing work which would otherwise have remained saved but not read. A great opportunity (given by Stephen).
> Barbara Gurney

first 10 years of GP's operation, the press published more than 450 books, thus giving about 400 writers the chance to experience a significant event in their life.

To celebrate the milestone, Stephen organised a two-day event on 1 and 2 July 2006 at Havelock House, Canberra, with a series of book-related discussions, author talks, readings and book launches, featuring authors from the ACT and interstate.

One of the books launched at the event was the anthology *On Common Water*, edited by Michael Byrne, which featured the work of 50 GP poets who had been published in the preceding decade. Commenting on GP's milestone, an article in *The Chronicle* stated that 'When any small business reaches its tenth anniversary, it's a cause for celebration,

The first sight of Ginninderra Press's cover of my biography stunned me: silence, then tears, as Stephen's design had me looking directly into the eyes of my subject.
Christine Ingleton

but in the tough world of publishing it's even more remarkable.'[5] Stephen added that GP's chance of succeeding was even more unique because 'It's small, unsubsidised, independent, and specialises in manuscripts that don't fit into the mainstream.'[6]

Although Stephen did not know what 'ginninderra' meant when he named the publishing house, he was quoted as saying during the 10th birthday events that he thought the press had lived up to its meaning 'by throwing out little rays of light'.[7]

Celebrations for GP's 10th anniversary were also held in the Dame Joan Sutherland Centre at St Catherine's Anglican Girls' School in Waverley, Sydney, where events included a panel discussion on the future of books. Further events were held at Ulverstone, Tasmania, with a book launch and Stephen giving a presentation about GP and the publishing world, and what publishers look for in manuscripts.

Moving on

After 23 years living in Canberra and 12 years after GP had begun, Stephen's life and GP were about to undergo an enormous upheaval. In his honest manner, Stephen reflected,

> My then-wife and I became estranged and I was faced with having to decide whether to stay in Canberra, or to change locations entirely. Since I had family in Adelaide, and had published quite a few South Australian authors, I decided that this might be a hospitable place to call home.

The difficulties of relocating on both a personal and professional level still astounds Stephen to this day.

> It was another Matthews headlong step into the unknown. I had no idea what would happen. It took a month to pack and unpack all the accumulated infrastructure of printing machines, computers, plus the loads of books, and then to set up new phone numbers and Internet providers. Logistically it was enormous, plus on the domestic front I, with the help of my family, had to find a new place to live that would also serve as an office for GP. However, in my blind way, I just assumed it would work out. There would have been no point in me thinking that maybe it couldn't. It had to.

At a farewell held for Stephen at Gorman House in Canberra, tributes flowed for Stephen's community spirit, especially his work during the Canberra bushfires. Author Craig Cormick said at the time that the company and its owner would be

---

Ginninderra Press has been an inspiration. Having my book of poetry chosen to be published has inspired me as a poet and has enthused me in my writing.
Colleen Keating

sadly missed. Craig said the move would negatively affect the Canberra literary community and make it harder for Canberra people to publish their works and access feedback for their manuscripts.[8]

In his optimistic manner, Stephen did not believe GP's move to Adelaide would adversely affect the ACT's literary scene. He noted that his move was not the end of the story but rather a new chapter in his life.

On learning of GP's relocation from the ACT to South Australia, Stephen received a letter from Jon Stanhope wishing to thank Stephen for his long-standing commitment to ACT-based writers and noting Stephen's significant contribution to the cultural life of Australia.

> No one would know better than yourself that it is a considerable achievement to operate a small press in today's economic, cultural and social climate. That you have managed to be successful for twelve years is even more impressive. That you have been successful despite a primary focus on mostly unknown writers is extraordinary…it is people like yourself who make a direct contribution to writing in Australia by giving writers the chance for their work to be produced, read, and – with just a bit of luck – reviewed.[10]

Reflecting on the move, Stephen believes GP has been able to successfully transfer from its Canberra base to Adelaide. He states that in some ways he can look back on those first 12 years in Canberra and regret the media connections he lost in moving – the newspapers and ABC radio – but there are other ways in which he believes the past eight years have been the best.

> Two things that in different ways have compensated for the media connections that haven't been replicated in Adelaide are the Tea Tree Gully Library and East Avenue Books. The Tea Tree Gully Library provides the most extraordinary support for the press and our authors, and other authors as well. They hold book launches, handle the publicity, cater for the events and give authors a bottle of wine with a label reproducing the cover of their book. No other library I've encountered does this. Also, East Avenue Books willingly supports the press in several ways – by stocking our books and by hosting author launches and book-related events – and there's simply not a shop like it in Canberra.

However, Stephen will readily state that the most significant reason for his happiness at the relocation of GP has been meeting the wonderful Brenda and finding a partner who shares, understands and helps in the operations of the press.

My first two books were published by GP and I'll be ever grateful for the opportunity. Thank you Brenda and Stephen for your warmth, hospitality and friendship over the years.
Sharon Kernot

I knew the first time I met Brenda in October 2008 that she was somebody special. A friend of Brenda's brought a manuscript to me, probably three months after I arrived. I accepted the manuscript but then she disappeared for a while. It was probably another three months before I saw her again. But when she resurfaced, it all fell into place. I was thrilled to publish her first book – *The Silver Cord*, a collection of poetry – early in 2009, as it was a passionate, heartfelt exploration of grief.

For the first 15 months Stephen and Brenda were together, Brenda was still working but after she retired from the Public Service and had some rest time, she joined Stephen in the day-to-day operation of the press. Stephen is thrilled that Brenda slipped so easily into the role of not only helping to get manuscripts ready for publication but also providing emotional support.

Most importantly, Brenda brought her wonderful customer service rapport that I'm not very good at. Also, the knowledge she has of writing and being published gives her a special insight. I can see all that at an intellectual level and understand it but Brenda has made me feel it. She has the capacity to appreciate other people's work and to understand how they're feeling during the publication process.

Involving himself in the community was something Stephen wanted to continue in Adelaide. He wanted to connect with writers, readers and the general literary community. Shortly after arriving in Adelaide, Stephen contacted the South Australian Writers' Centre and with the enthusiastic help of Jude Aquilina was able to use the centre as a base to meet with writers who had a manuscript ready for publication. Stephen met about 12 authors and as a result he accepted many of their manuscripts for publication. Jude then launched *Tiger! Tiger!*, a collection of stories by long-time GP author, Zenda Vecchio, and Stephen was grateful for Jude's hospitable words.

Jude was very effusive and positive and made me feel very welcome. I knew then that everything would work out for GP in Adelaide.

Stephen held readings in various locations

> GP is competent, reliable and very easy to work with. It's been wonderful seeing my short story collection, novel and selected poems going into print with such a professional publisher.
> Myra King

around Adelaide with some of his authors and poets, as well as meeting local writing groups, like the North East Writer's (NEWInc). As a result of Stephen meeting South Australian authors, he started receiving more manuscripts and publishing local writers who had not previously been published. Many of these authors have gone on to publish multiple books in several genres, including poetry, short story, novels and non-fiction.

Branching out

By 2011, GP was firmly entrenched in Adelaide and continued to be flooded with manuscripts from local and interstate writers. However, a new development was about to occur for GP inspired by an idea from long-time GP-published poet Ann Nadge – formerly of Sydney and now residing back in her home town of Adelaide. Ann has a particular love of The Cedars, the family home of acclaimed artist Hans Heysen. Ann suggested to Stephen the idea of gathering a group of GP's South Australian poets to meet at The Cedars and have them respond in verse to the art and studios of Hans Heysen and his daughter Nora. And for the poets to also explore the life of the other members of the Heysen family, including Hans's talented wife Sallie, as well as the interior and exterior of The Cedars and the tranquil surroundings of the tree-infused property in Hahndorf.

The result was *That Which My Eyes See*, edited by Ann and with delicate pencil drawings by artist, Kevin Stead, which contains 50 poems by 14 GP poets. The curator of The Cedars, Allan Campbell, who launched the collection early in May 2011, wrote in the book's preface,

> This delightful compilation of poems by the South Australian Ginninderra Press poets serves to continue the acknowledged presence of poetry as an identified and treasured element of family life at The Cedars. The

Thank you for believing in my work enough to publish me. It has truly changed the trajectory of my life. I now have a purpose and a belief in myself.
Dominic Kirwan

works selected, along with Kevin Stead's drawings, capture the unique spirit of this very special place.[11]

The rich history of Port Adelaide, GP's home, became the focus for the next anthology by GP authors and poets. Port Adelaide is a very special place to Stephen and Brenda and they were keen to adapt Ann's idea for *That Which My Eyes See* for a collection that embraced the past, present and future of the Port, in both creative fiction, and non-fiction pieces. Twenty-eight GP authors and poets spent time at the Port exploring the diversity of the area that is steeped not only in maritime history but in the colourful people who populated its past.

Brenda edited the collection, which featured 65 contributions, including poems, short stories and prose pieces. *The Heart of Port Adelaide* was launched by the Mayor of Port Adelaide, Gary Johanson, in November 2011. Tim Lloyd wrote in *The Advertiser* that the book is an anthology of writers' memories, histories and contemplation of the Port. The writers 'celebrate the wharves, the wool stores, boat sheds, pubs and the people. Modern experiences of tourism and dolphins and restoration of maritime history are set alongside nostalgic recollections through the eyes of great-great-grand-descendants.'[12]

Following on from these successful models that Stephen said 'have given opportunities for people to get together and create a sense of community', a new idea took shape in discussions between Brenda and Stephen. More ambitious in scope than the previous two creative anthologies, the new project would see GP's South Australian authors and poets approached to contribute to *Collecting Writers*. Forty-two authors and poets responded to the idea to write about what they collect, either in the form of poetry, fiction or non-fiction. *Collecting Writers* was launched by poet Graham Rowlands at the Tea Tree Gully Library in July 2013.

I first appreciated Ginninderra Press through David Campbell's marvellous Monaro poems. Subsequently I was deeply grateful for their encouragement and willingness to take on a plainly Christian poet. Happy Birthday!
Adrian Lane

The result is a cornucopia of more than 80 contributions featuring everything from tales of collecting wrapping paper, cats, biscuit tins, electrical insulators, keys, rejection notices to aprons, and even fragments of lives. In the introduction to the collection, Stephen noted,

> Over 40 writers – all resident in South Australia – reflect on the gamut of collecting, collectors and collections. All of them are *collecting* writers, whether they enjoy collecting tangibles like shells or spoons or books, or savour intangibles like words or memories or images… Since 1996, Ginninderra Press has in a way been collecting *writers*, especially ones with interesting and important things to say. It's a collection I've gathered with as much discernment and satisfaction as any collector of stamps or coins or scarves.[13]

Stephen acknowledges that two of the anthologies – *That What My Eyes See* and *The Heart of Port Adelaide* – have had disappointing sales, though he is heartened that almost all of the 300 copies printed of *Collecting Writers* were sold. However, Stephen has chosen to look at the positive outcomes of these anthologies.

> The three anthologies were successful in terms of creating a sense of community among the GP writers and making them feel part of what Brenda calls the 'GP family'. Also, if you're going to ask were these anthologies worth doing, yes of course they were, because we've ended up with, in all three cases, really important contributions to their subject matter. The Heysen anthology could be a model for any other similar institution to undertake, as it encapsulates a variety of responses to what people can see. In regard to *The Heart of Port Adelaide*, here's this endangered community and here was a way of drawing some threads back together. Anyone who reads the book would have a real glimpse of Port Adelaide's history and its present situation. Finally, *Collecting Writers* explored many aspects of what collecting means to people and what it involves. They're books to be proud of.

> Ginninderra Press's willingness to publish new voices has led to a richer, more diverse pool of writing in Australia. A wonderful achievement! I wish them many more successful years.
> *Gary MacRae*

Chapbooks

Mindful of the need to keep GP evolving and reinventing itself to stay relevant in the 21st century, the time was right in August 2014 for Stephen to embark on a new project that would reinvigorate both the press and himself. Stephen believes as a publisher he needs to be awake to and responsive to what is going on around him and alert to all sorts of possibilities.

> I never start out and say this is what I'm going to do because once you start doing that you're closing your eyes to those opportunities that will come at you from left field.

Serendipity would see two GP writers within one week ask Stephen if he would consider accepting manuscripts for poetry chapbooks. Up until this point, he had not been interested in replicating the traditional chapbook format that was being used by other contemporary publishing houses.

Chapbooks are an early example of simply designed books believed to have been conceived in 16th century Europe and reaching their peak popularity in the 17th and 18th century. They were produced cheaply in small, paper-covered booklets on a single sheet folded into books of 8, 12, 16 or 24 pages. The actual term was first recorded in English in 1824, and is thought to derive from the word 'chapman' for the itinerant salesmen who would sell such books.

> When I was approached, I started looking at the concept of chapbooks again and thought, what is it that I don't like about the format currently being used and what could I do to make them different? I wanted to find a point of difference – I wanted to make them more economical in shape and I wanted them to look distinctive. The size I chose meant that they could fit perfectly into a business-size envelope. Writers grasped this and the format made them more user-friendly, more promotable and easier to post.

Stephen is astonished at the speed with which the series known as Pocket Poets was embraced by GP writers and poetry readers. After agreeing to the idea in August 2014, GP had 30 titles by the December of that year, with sales in excess of 1,500.

After witnessing the response to Pocket Poets and the enthusiasm with which poets responded to them, it occurred to Stephen that the Pocket concept could be expanded upon.

> I was conscious of the fact that with *Voice* not existing there were expressions of opinion that didn't have the same outlet. Pocket Polemics occurred to me – I thought, let's have

---

Ginninderra Press has given me the opportunity to grow from an isolated childhood with only close family, to a public validation of my thoughts and acceptance into another family.
Jean McArthur

a series where people could let off steam about pet topics and this idea was quickly embraced by writers. In quick succession came Pocket People and Pocket Places, which were suggested out of the similar collegiate process where a group of similarly creative people see further opportunities for the expansion of the series that suit the format. With prose, the 5,000 word limit is a good length for authors. The three prose spin-offs from Pocket Poets have appealed to me as a continuation not only of what GP is about, but how they connect back to the material produced in *Voice*.

To May 2016, 46 Pocket Poets have been published by poets from across Australia. Five Pocket Polemics – with topics ranging from euthanasia to James Joyce have been produced. Nine Pocket Places have explored everywhere from inner Canberra to Forty Green in England, and six Pocket People featuring stories about writers' family members have been published. Total Pocket sales have reached 3,770.

Bright spark

Towards the end of 2014 an even more significant development was to occur in the history of GP and change the way it had operated since its inception. Late in October, Stephen received an email from Debbie Lee, the Manager, Content Acquisition, at Ingram Spark, a print-on-demand business, who was coming to Adelaide to explore future business opportunities. After looking at GP's website, Debbie realised she knew Stephen from her days as a sales representative for Random House 25 years ago. At a dinner meeting, Debbie explained to Stephen and Brenda how Spark operated their print on demand system for printed books and ebooks, and she also outlined Spark's ability to automatically distribute the books through Amazon, the Book Depository and other sales channels.

Stephen could see the huge potential in linking GP to Spark but wanted to test the system for himself. He needed a guinea pig, and as usual that involved Brenda, who had written five collections of non-fiction books about life by the Port River and her travels around Australia. Stephen thought this could be an opportunity to gather them into the one volume and try the whole Spark process. In November, he started the process by getting the copy ready and re-editing the material into one volume. Just before Christmas 2014, Stephen had uploaded the file and the first printed copy of *From Patagonia to Australia* arrived early in January 2015. The result according to Stephen was 'brilliant'.

Being published rarely brings fortunes but it does give a writer credibility. We have felt encouraged to continue to explore unique ways of expressing our thoughts and feelings.
Max and Jacqui Merckenschlager.

We were staggered by the quality of the printed book, and the speed and ease of the process and its worldwide availability. People have been talking about print on demand systems for at least as long as GP's history but nobody had ever been able, that I knew of, to make it possible to print just one or two copies at a price that would make it work for a publisher to make any money. Somehow Spark is able to print single copies at a cost that does make it viable. They make it much easier for us to print copies that we want locally, but we're now seeing them being available to be printed in the UK, US and anywhere worldwide. We've even been selling quantities of ebooks that we hadn't been able to do before. It's like a dream come true.

Stephen acknowledges that working with Spark has been very significant in GP's evolution. In the space of just 12 months, Stephen noted that important and beneficial changes were in place.

Printing on demand for one thing means that we no longer have boxes and boxes of books needing to be stored. The usual print run of the previous system was 200 copies but now we only ever need to order the exact number of books that we want – it doesn't matter if we order two copies or 200. Because the turnaround time is so fast, we can receive books within a week of ordering them. So that means there aren't so many boxes to store and move because the local printer we used would deliver boxes here, and then we had to take them to store elsewhere because there's no room to leave them here. We had to be constantly rearranging our shelves in the store because of the books going in and out. We save huge amounts of time now. Also, we no longer need to produce the thermal-bound books because producing small quantities is easily viable through Spark. The best thing is that the quality of the printed product is brilliant.

Stephen firmly believes he has always followed his instincts in operating GP without a great deal of conscious thinking.

I'm happy following my instincts. I didn't dwell much at the time on the fact that it was called Spark but that turned out to be apt, because it has regenerated GP – it has given a spark to the whole business. There's the significance of the meaning of 'spark', and 'ginninderra' meaning 'throwing out rays of light', so it's all interconnected – if there is

I am grateful that Stephen came to Australia to do what it seems we can't do for ourselves: side-step government control of funding and give regional writers a fair go.
Tim Metcalf

some master plan in the back of my head, then maybe I realised that at the time. That might have been why I found the idea so attractive.

However, being committed to the needs of other people, Stephen did face a difficult decision due to his having made a virtue of being a small, locally based independent publisher.

> The only real sticking point for me was that this meant transferring my business from a local small printer to a huge global conglomerate and although the printer we used certainly didn't depend for its survival on us, nonetheless they'd be losing quite some thousands of dollars. But in the end the difference between what they could offer and what Spark could offer was too vast to ignore – that whole connection to global possibilities of books being bought anywhere in the world and thus found on websites from the UK to Germany to Japan, and for that to be enmeshed in a whole price structure that was more affordable, was just too good to ignore in the end.

Another unforeseen difficulty Stephen faced in the process of GP's conversion from a conventional print model to the print on demand system was having to deal with many boxes full of unsold books. Authors were given the option of having their books converted to the print on demand system and thereby making them available for purchase from worldwide websites, and as ebooks. As part of that process, they were given the option of collecting their unsold books or having them pulped.

> I found this process very distressing. These are books authors had spent considerable time over and I had accepted them readily and had the belief they were books worthy of being published. Also, I had spent many hours editing them and preparing them for publication. In the previous system we had to print at least 200 copies to make it economically viable. Their failure to sell had absolutely nothing to do with the quality of the work. The whole process for authors and me of having these unsold boxes of books is the burial of hopes and dreams.

Picaro Press

Putting this disappointment aside, the need for GP to be constantly evolving, and opening itself up to new possibilities, has always been at the forefront of Stephen's mind. Indeed, new opportunities were again in the offing in April 2015, when Stephen noticed a post on Facebook indicating that Rob Riel of Picaro Press was

> Stephen Matthews's acceptance of my first book for publishing was a life-changing moment. My lasting relationship with Ginninderra Press is based on their constant encouragement, my appreciation and mutual friendship.
> *Helen Mitchell*

seeking a new owner for his business. Stephen quickly sent Rob an email noting that GP and Picaro Press might be compatible. Although Rob had other people making enquiries about taking over Picaro, he said, 'Yes, let's do it' to Stephen straight away. It took slightly longer than it would normally have because Rob was caught up in the huge storms that were raging around the NSW central coast at the time. However, he eventually sent Stephen all the files and the ownership of the business name.

Stephen had to decide the best way to merge GP's new Picaro publications with Rob's previous publishing, which included full-length collections of poetry and chapbooks.

> After much thought, Picaro Poets came into being – we designed new chapbooks in the poetry series keeping the Picaro name. Also, we have reprinted some original Picaro Press titles and published some new titles that had not quite been finished when the takeover occurred. Brenda was appointed the series editor of the Picaro Poets series and we had an extremely successful launch of the series by poet Jill Gower at East Avenue Books in September 2015. Sales have been very good and they are attracting a new group of poets who are keen to be published under the Picaro Press imprint, and some of these poets are likely to go on to publish a full-length collection under the GP imprint. The reaction to the look of the chapbooks has been extremely positive – people like their parchment covers and vellum flyleaves.

Stephen believes that the acquisition of another highly thought of poetry publisher is a very noteworthy event in GP's history and he feels immense pride in what this means for his press.

> I believe it's indicative of GP reaching some kind of maturity that we were able to do this. It's sad that there's essentially one less publisher for poets to send their work to, but for GP it's part of that whole new burst of energy that's occurred since 2014. It's part of GP's reframing, redefining and restructuring. Here we are getting that burst of energy, getting that spark and the good thing is that the Picaro name will continue – quite a good result for their 14 years.

Stephen is often asked why he keeps publishing poetry when there is already so much that has been published, dating back centuries, and surely every subject that exists has already been written about. Stephen has always been quick to respond to this question.

The wise children's author Patricia Wrightson once said to me that she had thought there

---

I have experienced the thrill of seeing my poems published many times before, but my own poetry collection by Ginninderra Press was a highlight.
Jill Nevile

was nothing new to write about and she was quite distressed by that. However, when flying to Tasmania, she looked out of the window and thought, the poet John Keats had never flown in a plane! Poetry is the oldest form of written expression and it requires of its reader a stillness – a slowness for people to absorb it and reflect. People don't get many opportunities to do this – we're encouraged to be on the go, to make quick choices.

The importance of poetry in society was supported by ACT Chief Minister Stanhope in 2005 when launching two GP poetry collections. He noted the 'profound influence poetry can have on the public understanding of contemporary issues…and that poetry has the ability to effect social, political and cultural change'.[14]

Similarly, Stephen has been questioned about his desire to publish short stories. However, his support for this writing genre received much praise from *The Age* reviewer Dianne Dempsey in 2009:

> In an era when the short story is as fashionable as flying ducks, small presses such as Ginninderra are to be congratulated for supporting this satisfying but almost extinct art form.[15]

Further praise was recorded by *Tasmanian Town & Country* reviewer Ian Kennedy Williams:

> Ginninderra Press has probably done more than any [publisher] to promote the writing and publication of a form that has been a significant part of the Australian literary landscape since Henry Lawson began publishing his stories in the old *Bulletin*.[16]

The publishing process

Acquiring Picaro, producing the chapbooks, and the new Spark association have made life for Brenda and Stephen

STORIES

Storms
Ian Wilkinson
Ginninderra Press, $18
Reviewer *Dianne Dempsey*

I'M NOT sure why but there seems to be more people writing short stories these days than there are reading them. It's a pity the genre is no longer popular because it can deliver a mighty punch of pleasure. It is also an important training ground for writers.

With each of Ian Wilkinson's short stories we see him flex his literary muscles. We watch how he weaves his way back and forward in time, how sharp his dialogue is and how skilfully he can take us to a particular place.

Wilkinson's strength is his background as an architect. Where we live, or where we choose to live, defines us. In *The Man Who Met Raymond Carver* a young girl who grew up in a dilapidated weatherboard terrace stays with her boyfriend, not for love or his money but for his beautiful house. The house is a "large ship-like structure" by the sea. "If he lost the house, I'd be off," she says. In *Dark Blue* a girl mourns the death of a former boyfriend who loved the sea. She asks, "why did he have to, die at a place like Shepparton, for God's sake?"

In an era when the short story is as fashionable as flying ducks, small presses such as Ginninderra are to be congratulated for supporting this satisfying but almost extinct art form.

> With GP you know that if you observe the publisher's guidelines your work will be judged on its merits; and that, in today's difficult market conditions, means a great deal.
> *Adrian Rogers*

even busier than it was before, if that is possible. Presiding over such a full-time hands-on business for two people requires many skills, including extensive up-to-date printing and publishing knowledge, slick organisational skills, streamlined systems, passion, energy and a belief in what you are doing – Stephen and Brenda operate GP with the afore-mentioned expertise in abundance.

Spend any time with this indefatigable duo and you become exhausted watching them perform their daily tasks. They each know their place, and work in a respectful, collaborative and coordinated manner. Stephen works in the downstairs office at the rear of their home, with two desktop computers and three printers buzzing around him – though amusingly with all his high-tech equipment he has a very basic-looking home-made press that requires a degree of force to be used in the hands-on production of the Pocket and Picaro chapbooks. Meanwhile, Brenda is in her upstairs studio with a view of the river as she works tirelessly on her computer preparing manuscripts for publication, responding to emails, and assessing the poetry manuscripts she receives – and thus deciding whether to accept or reject them.

Stephen is quick to stress that although operating his publishing house is something he and Brenda are passionate about, it is not a get rich quick scheme. In fact, he notes that keeping a regular cash flow to sustain the business has only been made slightly easier due to his receiving small sums from his English and Australian pensions in the past few years. Usually, he adds, GP makes a small profit but never enough to pay a mortgage or bring up a family. Another publishing myth Stephen is quick to defuse is the notion that publishers are caught up in a whirl of prestige.

> People think publishing is surrounded by glamour, when really a lot of it is humdrum stuff. Our working day starts at about 8 a.m. when we check our respective emails from authors or customers, then we check at the post office for new manuscripts, orders or payments, or to post out books. Then it's back home to process orders. The tricky part is there is so much administrative work that you sometimes feel that a large part of the day is gone before you're able to look at the books that are in the pipeline – that you may have started to lay out, edit, or be entering corrections; all the things that are moving the business along and are part of the creative process. Also, we often need to go out and stock up on stationery and equipment, things I hasten to add we both like! However, they are distractions to the publishing process. Our working day usually finishes at about 4 p.m., when we might go for a bike ride or a walk. We don't operate the press on a Monday to Friday basis but work seven days a week if we need to.

> When a poet wants to publish a book
> Ginninderra Press is the place to look
> With Brenda and Stephen on your side
> Your words will be published with pride!
> *Margaret Reichardt*

The glamorous allure of publishing is no doubt the result of people hearing about the magical stories of publishers receiving a manuscript that has the wow factor and becomes a publishing phenomenon in the vein of the Harry Potter novels. Stephen not only is adverse to the idea of entering this world, but admits very few manuscripts he receives have that X factor. However, he is quick to add that being sent the diaries of a World War I soldier by one of his surviving sons early in GPs formative years was very significant and exciting for him. So impressed was Stephen with these diaries that he decided to be the editor on the project and the result was the acclaimed book *Not Theirs The Shame Who Fight: Selections from the World War 1 diaries, poems and letters of Private R.C. (Cleve) Potter*, published in 1999.

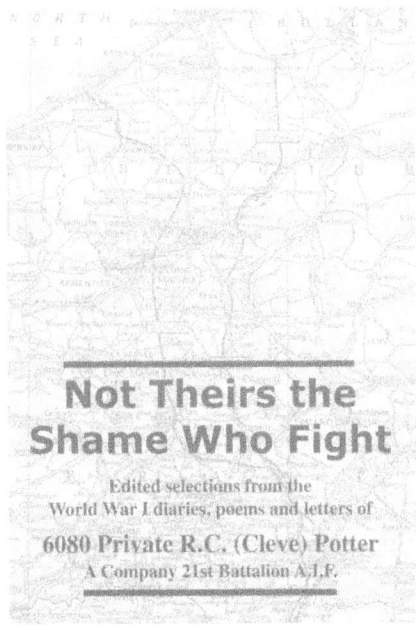

> The moment I held the original handwritten World War I diaries of Private Potter, who was from New England in NSW, was very memorable. This manuscript appealed to me from a general historical point of view, a poetry point of view and the fact that I'm interested in the First World War. It is certainly a highlight of my publishing career and it was widely praised.

Reviewing the book in *Panorama* magazine in *The Canberra Times*, in 1999, John Farquharson wrote,

> Matthews is to be commended for editing and publishing these diaries, poems and letters, which have a haunting, memorable quality. In doing so he has given us a jewel of First World War literature.[17]

In the early days, GP received up to 20 unsolicited manuscripts a week but this has decreased in the past few years to about five to 10 a week. The reason, according to Stephen, is that it is much easier for people to make initial enquiries by email to ask if GP would be interested in publishing their work. The guidelines on GP's website also

---

Ginninderra Press – the chance to meet, and appreciate,
Stephen and Brenda; for what more could a writer ask?
John Sabine

state clearly what the press publishes, and that it does not accept manuscripts aimed at the children's market or novels from authors not previously published by the press.

However, receiving anywhere between 250 and 500 manuscripts a year requires an enormous amount of time to be set aside for reading.

> I usually wait until there are at least 10 or 12 manuscripts in the in-tray and spend a weekend reading them. I can't do this on a casual basis; you need to set aside time and get the right head space because it's very different reading new manuscripts from doing screen work. I still, as far as possible, insist that people send in a hard-copy manuscript because I think that if something is going to end up on paper, then you need to assess how it's going to look on paper, and that requires reading it on paper. Reading on screen, even if you're trying to determine whether you want to publish something, is so different; you're not using the same part of your brain.

Of the vast number of manuscripts Stephen receives, he only accepts about 50 titles to publish a year. Stephen is reluctant to let authors know exactly what he is looking for in a manuscript.

> I don't like to think about it too much, as it would close my sensibilities down. Also, authors might only pitch something that they thought I was looking for, and that could be deadly dull.

In respect of the chapbooks in both the Pocket series and the Picaro series, GP receives a regular amount of manuscripts and they undergo the same selection criterion that applies to all of the GP manuscripts that are received. According to Stephen, the manuscripts seem to come in waves throughout the year and one of the reasons it is hard to give an exact number is that their arrival is quite affected by the time of the year. He notes that

> It's always interesting that that there's a surge of manuscripts received at the beginning of February. Obviously people who have day jobs and have holidays during the festive season worked on their manuscripts and you get the result of that in February.

Interestingly, about 70 per cent of GP's top sellers (see table opposite) have been non-fiction books, and Stephen believes this is due to readers feeling there is less risk taking involved when buying factual books.

> When people are looking at what books they want to buy, what they want to read, what

---

Ginninderra Press has been a wonderful gift for many people – a most encouraging and welcoming fresh breeze, minimising the difficulties in publishing and motivating writers to share their work.
Ros Schulz

Title	Number sold	non-fiction	text	fiction	poetry
How did the fire know we lived here?	6749	✓			
Mary Cunningham	1503	✓			
Rainbow	1119	✓			
Mental health social work/Mental health practice	949		✓		
Floating in foyers	935	✓			
Framework of flesh	856	✓			
Catharine with an A	845	✓			
Chooks in the city	811	✓			
Not just footy (2 editions)	699	✓			
Not theirs the shame who fight	683	✓			
Hidden desires	655			✓	
The strength of us	649				✓
Journey with cancer	639	✓			
They liked me, the horses, straightaway	612	✓			
Farming ghosts	605			✓	
But what can I say?	601	✓			
Smoke and mirrors	579			✓	
Conflict management (2 editions)	558		✓		
How to succeed without really trying	523	✓			
Historic pubs around Sydney	514	✓			
Love affair with Australian literature	505	✓			
She's a fat tart, ain't she	505	✓			

they want to spend their money on, non-fiction books have an immediate yes or no response. Am I interested in this subject, yes or no? When people are deciding on buying a novel, that's a harder decision. You know when you look at a book of non-fiction, and you look at who wrote it, the question isn't, do I know this author, but do I want to learn more about the subject they're writing about? When you're looking at a novel by an author you mightn't know, you're taking a far bigger gamble.

Although not wanting to define what he looks for in a manuscript, Stephen is very clear about the skills a publisher needs:

You need lots of patience and a lot of sensitivity, as you're dealing with people's work and they put a lot of themselves into their writing. In a literary sense you have to have an appreciation of the literary culture. You need a sense of what has already been written

Thank you Ginninderra Press for accepting my writing into print and all small people like me whose writing you have accepted.
Alice Shore

about and where the gaps may be. You need to have a really good grasp of language and its mechanics. I maintain that you don't have to be a novelist yourself and you don't have to be a poet or a writer of any genre, but you do have to know how these different genres work. You have to love the language and have a good understanding of English grammar – the whole nuts and bolts of the English language, which I'm truly grateful I received as part of my education. All of that whole immersion in the culture of print is really important and that takes a long time to acquire.

As well as literary skills, Stephen notes that if you are going to be a small, independent publisher, then you also have to have the technological capabilities to be able to make the most of the software and you have to keep up with the changes in both software and hardware. Plus, he is quick to add that you have to be able to do all the drudgery as well – you have to be able to handle boxes, keep up with new postal changes and postage rates and much more.

Stephen's vast knowledge gained from his study and his extensive reading is put to good use in copy editing the manuscripts he has accepted to publish. This is one of the aspects of publishing he loves most.

> There's a huge satisfaction in editing, because one of the things you're doing is serving the intentions of the writer and the needs of the reader – making sure punctuation, grammar and formatting are right, without in many cases doing anything radical, makes a huge difference to the author's work. And if you get it right, it's almost an invisible art.

An important part of any book is its design and cover image, and this is a task Stephen undertakes for the majority of GP publications. In consultation with the author, Stephen selects the most appropriate image for the cover, whether it is a photograph, a drawing or a painting. As a lover of fonts, he carefully chooses the one he thinks best enhances the image. However, he is always keen to accommodate the wishes of authors who want to design their own book covers or who have friends or family members with these skills.

Stephen was thrilled to receive an email in 2015 from a bookseller in England after he received his order of a recent GP poetry book:

> I want to congratulate you on the whole design, feel and readability of the book… totally what all publishers should aspire to. Handling several hundred books a day it was obvious that a lot of care and thought had been put into it…well done![18]

Who thought a whisper
would echo and re-echo
half-way round the world?
Robin Sinclair

The careful editing of GP books and their design is crucial to the final product and when the finished book arrives in the hands of the author, they recognise the months of work that have gone into its creation. The author, naturally, is acutely aware of the months and often years that they have spent working on the book. Stephen believes publishers can become blasé about book publishing but since sharing his life with Brenda he has been able to see first-hand what it means to be published.

> Being with Brenda has reminded me more than anything else how significant getting published is – it really does change people's lives.

The celebration of the book's publication is never more keenly felt by the author than at the launches held for their book. Stephen and Brenda have criss-crossed Australia to share in the joy of publication for their authors. Stephen firmly believes that

> Launches are really important for authors. Some authors find them difficult but that's part of the process of coming out as a writer. It's exactly that – it's authors standing up and saying here I am, this is my book, which is part of the whole process of publication. It's an important declaration.

Stephen regrets that in the past 20 years he has not kept a journal of all the launches he has attended. GP launches have been held in galleries, libraries, bookshops, community halls and private homes. Country launches, he has found, usually attract the largest crowds. One of the largest Stephen has attended occurred in GP's early years and featured the launch of *Defenestration*, a debut collection by a young Canberra poet.

> She managed to get more than 100 people to attend and was confident she'd sell 100 copies of her book. I thought, oh right – I still had memories of when I was managing the Co-op bookshop in Canberra, and even in a large venue like that you'd be happy to sell 30 to 50 copies. It was a spectacular evening held at Gorman House, with a band as well. Towards the end of the evening she came to me and asked how many books were left. I said, 'You've sold 96.' She said, 'I'll fix that!' She went around finding out who hadn't bought a copy and by the end she did sell 100.

Throughout GP's 20 years, Stephen has chosen not to seek government subsidies to sustain the press. He believes going down this path would have compromised GP's independence:

> Ginninderra Press published my first three poetry books. They continue to sell today. Stephen was the first publisher to see something in my work – I'll always be grateful to him.
> *Melinda Smith*

In order to get subsidies, there are at least two inherent problems. Firstly, you have to make a case for the publishability of a book, to push its benefits, and that leaches out some of the specialness of it. If you're going to be an independent publisher, you've got to be independent. If you're then going to let someone else have a hand in deciding what you're publishing, then you've already given up a chunk of your independence. Secondly, the time involved in applying for grants is considerable, which means you can be waiting up to a year before you've been told if you're successful. If you have a manuscript that's topical, that can be too long to wait.

The importance Stephen places on GP maintaining its independence is firmly bound up with the books he publishes.

My choices of what to publish are not constrained in the same way as mainstream publishers who have to refer to a committee including marketing people who look at whether the book is going to make money. All the publishing decisions are made by Brenda and me – we can publish books that have some intrinsic value regardless of whether they'll make a lot of money.

Future words

Having recently celebrated his 70th birthday, Stephen had previously thought this milestone would see him slowing down. Interestingly, looking back through the GP archives at interviews with Stephen at the time of GP's 10th birthday celebrations, he stated quite firmly that he believed reaching the 20-year milestone in 2016 would be much harder to achieve.

We're trying to sell against huge multinationals, so it's not getting any easier. I think if we're here in another 10 years, that will be a great thing in itself.[19]

However, with all the recent developments that have occurred with Spark, the Picaro acquisition and the publication of the chapbooks, Stephen is looking firmly to the future with excitement and a renewed vigour. He is even optimistic that the printed book is no longer in danger of disappearing in the foreseeable future.

Two or three years ago, I thought that if ebooks continued to grow as quickly as they seemed to be then, the printed book might have a cloudy future. As a small publisher using the print on demand method, we would have been better placed than the large publishing houses because we could print in smaller numbers. However, the economics wouldn't stack

---

Never come across a more supportive, fuss-free publishing process, nor more talented graphic artists. Congratulations GP for providing such opportunity for writers and artists alike.
Steve Tolbert

up enough for the multinationals because the mass market works by printing loads of books and lots of copies so they can end up with a lower selling price. Now that people have a grasp of what ebooks are about, I think that for many people that may have clarified to them what printed books are all about. Ebooks have a definite place and a usefulness for people who have lots of books on their devices, whether they're commuters, or people on holidays who no longer have to carry piles of books with them. But people also have seen that there are still advantages with print in terms of its tangibility, durability or aesthetics. I'm more optimistic about the future of the printed book today.

Stephen's ongoing desire to keep GP at the forefront of social issues that are important to writers today, and his passion for producing anthologies that provide an outlet for the work of GP writers, coincided with plans for the press's 20th birthday celebrations. As part of the anniversary, a significant anthology, *First Refuge: Poems on Social Justice*, was launched on 2 July 2016 at the Tea Tree Gully Library.

The anthology, edited by Ann Nadge, was the result of a call to GP writers to submit poems on the theme of social justice. *First Refuge* contains 85 poems contributed by previously published GP authors and poets. Ann notes in the introduction to the book that 'Beyond the notion of GP's anniversary, Stephen Matthews was keen to capture and create a record of the social justice issues that, at this time in history, bring shame and hope to Ginninderra Press poets nationwide.'[20] Brenda adds that the books GP chooses to publish, of which *First Refuge* is a prime example, are the voices of Australia's conscience.

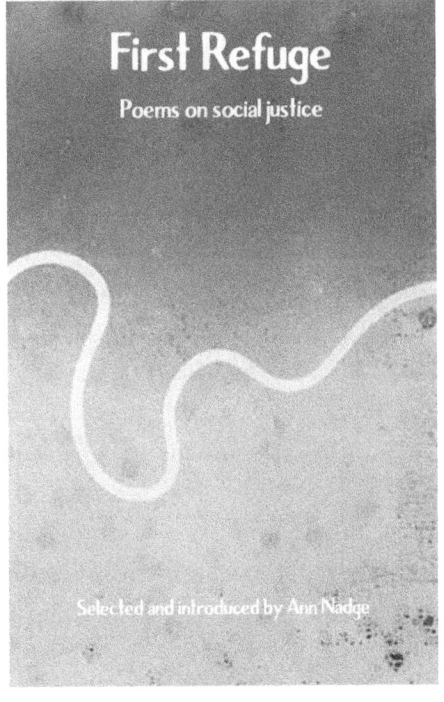

Coming full circle from his early days as a shy young man wanting a career in publishing to today celebrating the success of GP's first 20 years, Stephen concedes that in some ways he is grateful for what may in hindsight have been the wisdom of the careers guidance counselling who put him off publishing when he was 21.

The encouragement of Stephen, Brenda and Ginninderra Press has been instrumental in developing my writing life. These wonderful people and their press really do bring light to dark places.
Valerie Volk

I'm sure the reason he put me off was the English class system rather than his insight into my actual capabilities. But he probably did me a favour, as to be able to work in publishing you need to have gained experience in life and employment. The same applies to writers. There are too many pitfalls. Over the years so many high school or university students have wanted to do work experience or internships with GP and they all have the same kind of enthusiasm I had when I was young but they don't have the experience. Quite simply, they don't know what they don't know. They'll look at a piece of text and don't know where there's a misplaced hyphen or how to format dialogue. It is possible to teach these things but it's a slow process, with knowledge gained from extensive reading and practice.

Stephen believes what has driven his beloved press to continue over the past 20 years is his sheer 'bloody-mindedness' – even through financial hardships, personal upheavals, and the vast technological changes that have resulted in the need for the press to move into electronic publishing alongside the printed version. He is proud that GP has lasted for 20 years and has published work by hundreds of new writers whose lives have been changed for the better.

To be a part of something that allows somebody's voice to be transferred to the written page, and to share in the author's excitement, is huge. I've been determined to keep the press going since its inception in 1996. I won't be told what to publish or how to run the business. I have the luxury of making the decisions and I've always found a way of coping with the constrictions of the market. There's an element of survival there – this is mine, this is a part of me. I'll continue doing this because I must do it.

And indeed Stephen has done it, with the total number of GP books sold nearing 160,000. As previously stated, most of the books GP has published during the past 20 years have had small print runs of 200 copies but over 20 books have sold upwards of 500 copies, many reaching the 1,000 mark. To date, almost 70 Pockets and close to 30 Picaro Poets have been published. The total number of GP books published (including ebooks and Picaro Poets, but not Pockets) is about 1,200 – half of which are poetry books, and the other half equally divided between fiction and non-fiction.

Nelson Mandela said, '…as we let our own light shine, we unconsciously give other people permission to do the same'. With Stephen and Brenda at the helm, Ginninderra Press has been a beacon of light – publishing the work of writers throughout Australia and allowing light to shine on hundreds of authors and illuminate their words.

It was great to be published by a notable press such as GP, allowing me to showcase poems a little different in content than most publishers were willing to take on.
Gail Willems

References

1. All quotes from Stephen Matthews were recorded in face-to-face interviews conducted in 2010, 2015 and 2016, unless otherwise referenced.
2. Christopher Bantick, 'The vision behind Canberra voice', *The Canberra Times, Panorama*, 4 December 2004
3. Ibid.
4. Jennifer Moran, 'A fair question on fire launches 3,500 books', *The Canberra Times*, 30 April 2003
5. 'Canberra Publisher turns 10', *The Chronicle*, Canberra, 11 July 2006
6. Stephanie Gardiner, 'Celebrating a decade of publishing', *The Canberra Times*, 1 July 2006
7. Ibid.
8. Ewa Kretowicz, 'A new chapter begins for Canberra publisher', *The Canberra Times*, 26 May 2008
9. Ibid.
10. Letter from ACT Chief Minister Jon Stanhope, 1 July 2008
11. Allan Campbell, Curator of The Cedars, Ann Nadge (ed.), *That Which My Eyes See*, Ginninderra Press, Adelaide, 2011
12. Tim Lloyd, 'Memories of grand days at Port', *The Advertiser*, Adelaide, 24 March 2012
13. Stephen Matthews, in Brenda Eldridge (ed.), *Collecting Writers*, Ginninderra Press, Adelaide, 2013
14. Catherine Naylor, 'For writers, war and peace proves to be pure poetry, *The Canberra Times*, 31 January 2005
15. Dianne Dempsey reviewing *Storms*, by Ian Wilkinson, *The Age*, Melbourne, 21 March 2009
16. Ian Kennedy Williams reviewing *Agony & Variations: Stories*, by Robert Cox, Tasmanian Town and Country, 2011
17. John Farquharson, 'War Genre Gem', *The Canberra Times, Panorama*, 5 June 1999
18. Email from English bookseller to Stephen Matthews, 13 August 2015
19. 'Canberra Publisher Turns 10', op. cit.
20. Ann Nadge (ed.), *First Refuge: Poems on Social Justice*, Ginninderra Press, Adelaide, 2016

GP publishing my poetry provided an opportunity to present myself to people as a writer and to answer questions as a writer – valuable experience if my novel is accepted for publication.

Adriana Wood

Stones Across a River

Thérèse Corfiatis
Tasmanian poet

The ancient art of writing verse is a powerful medium, where life's observations and reflective moments can be condensed into a small space.

My first book of poetry, *Seasons of the Soul*, was written with Anne Landers and published by Ginninderra Press in 2000. Anne and I met by accident, in a way – both of us were mothers of young people with disabilities, and although it was my support work concerning her daughter that drew us together, we later found many connections at other levels…and writing was the common denominator. Interestingly, we were born and raised in Hobart, but now found ourselves living on Tasmania's north-west coast. How we got to be there could well prove to be a novel in the making!

We eventually decided to collaborate and self-publish our own poetry. We were like children entering a strange, new dimension. Neither of us had the knowledge nor marketing skills necessary, although Anne's computer expertise saw her print out the first copy of the book we intended to launch into the world. She worked very hard on it; the end result looked quite professional and attractive. However, we soon realised it would be difficult and expensive to do ourselves. This led to a decision to approach Tasmanian publishers as an alternative. All our efforts came to no avail.

Anne googled various publishing houses on the mainland, and came across Ginninderra Press (GP), which was based in the ACT at that time. We liked the social justice component, and the fact that unknown writers had been given a go. We knew how difficult it was to get poetry published, and how hard it was for the small writer to have a voice.

We liked the fact that GP chose to operate without any direct subsidies from the public purse. They also provided opportunities for emerging writers in unfashionable genres or on unpopular subjects. GP offered to publish manuscripts it believed had merit, and also recognised that there were many more publishable manuscripts than mainstream publishers could publish. I am, in fact, directly quoting from one of their information pamphlets.

We sent off a submission with a covering letter that sounded like a war cry. Imagine our joy when Stephen Matthews contacted us to say he was interested in our work. We did a little dance together and felt totally vindicated. Anne felt stifled by family and friends who didn't take her writing very seriously, and I felt afraid, because all my writing, from about the age of 10, had been done in total isolation. Suddenly our work would be out there. It had changed everything.

Our first book spoke to a sense of place. Both Anne and I had lived away from Tasmania for a long time, and then returned to it after upheavals in our lives. We felt rejuvenated by its magnificent and ever-changing landscape.

We enjoyed the peace and solitude; in fact, Anne's earlier life had seen her living on both Tasman Island and Eddystone Point lighthouses. My poems for *Seasons of the Soul* were written in a quiet, seaside town with a small population, surrounded by awe-inspiring beauty. My reconnection to place catapulted me back into a spirituality that had always existed within. I was home on my beloved island, with its shimmering, clear skies and haunting landscape. My other life, with all its heartache, was beginning to heal at last.

The words flowed in a way they had not done for decades. I managed to carve out time for writing, setting up a place on the enclosed front veranda of the rented house I lived in. When I went there, my family knew to leave me alone.

A dear friend, who understood how important my writing was, helped organise the veranda's transformation. Why hadn't I thought of doing this before? With the manic pace of a carer's life, this simple solution just never occurred to me. Sometimes others can see what we need, before we do. She encouraged me to keep my reference books and writing tools at hand. I became more disciplined about devoting myself seriously to the word. The end result was a new book of poetry about to be offered to the world – *Seasons of the Soul*.

Christopher Bantick wrote in the *Sunday Examiner*'s book review on 5 March 2000,

> The enduring quality of this collection is the centrality of Tasmania to the poems. Both Landers and Corfiatis write of the 'terraced town of Hobart' as being highly significant on their later lives. This is a timely collection. Not only do the poems announce Tasmania's wild beauty but it is the connection between the geography of the soul and setting which speaks to us of the changes and chances of this fleeting world.

We had arrived as poets.

It had taken decades for both Anne and myself to be recognised for what we always knew we were – women poets whose craft had shaped our lives and separate journeys. It was also the mechanism by which we both survived the obstacles faced along the way.

Anne and I firmly believed poetry was losing its importance in the modern world. The ancient art of writing verse is a powerful medium, where life's observations and reflective moments can be condensed into a small space. We wished to share our thoughts; our hopes, joys and fears with the reader, and become a catalyst for a flowering of wider awareness. In a sense, GP provided a launching pad for our combined passion, and we hoped this could serve as an example to other women writers, especially those in rural areas.

With this aim in mind, Anne and I felt motivated enough to start up a women writers' group in Ulverstone in 1999. It had many changes of venue, but now operates out of the West Ulverstone Community House each month. After a democratic naming process put to a vote, the group is now known as Sunday Scribblers. In 2006, the group received financial assistance from the Women Tasmania grant to self-publish its first anthology, *Journey into Words*.

There has been a flowering of talent and confidence since then, with members' work accepted for radio and publication. GP published our oldest writer, at the age of 87. What an incredible achievement for a regional writers' group!

But I digress somewhat! Anne and I were proud to be able to present our book to the people of the north-west coast of Tasmania on a blue-skied, blustery day. A wild foaming sea roared into the shore, not less than 200 metres away – a dramatic backdrop for such a memorable occasion in our lives.

It was launched in Penguin by the Central Coast Mayor, Mike Downie (now deceased), on Sunday 12 March 2000 at the Lions Penguin Festival. Anne and I spoke individually; I thanked those who had come especially for the launch, but I was so nervous, I couldn't read. Anne did it for me. Now, with five more collections to my name, and a Pocket Poets chapbook as well, I have learnt to control my anxiety about reading in public.

Seasons of the Soul was a pivotal moment in my life. It was satisfying when people contacted me to say how much they liked a certain poem, and why it resonated with them. My work was connecting to the wider public, and that was all I had ever wanted.

The publishing process itself has been a learning curve. At first, it was daunting and all-consuming. We needed to proofread and edit our own work, and make decisions about what poems to keep in, or remove, due to the format agreed upon with the publisher.

As I moved on to write further collections, I learnt the necessary steps in the process, and it became easier with each submission. I would post off my hard copy, double-spaced, to Stephen Matthews, and wait six to eight weeks for a response. If accepted, I then posted an electronic version on a CD to him. I would then receive my first proof in the mail, and edit carefully, checking spelling and grammar with a fine-tooth comb. Indeed, I have been particularly fortunate to have a writing friend who willingly gave her time and effort to help me do this. An extra set of eyes and a fresh mind works wonders! So there is a bit of give and take, but to receive the first copy of the book, with its cover, and my name under its title, was an amazing feeling.

Many hundreds of hours go into writing poetry. Choosing a collection to eventually send away is difficult and all-consuming. Would I choose the right work? Would the reading public think it worthy? Waiting anxiously for a response is part of the whole experience. To have a manuscript accepted leaves one in a euphoric state for days! It did for me, at any rate.

I have a real sense of loyalty to GP. There is honest communication between us, and authentic mentorship and friendship. Over the past 15 years, and with a further five books published, one cannot help but form a close and endearing bond with the publisher who has helped it all happen.

Stephen is amazing; if I sent an email to ask something, he replied promptly. He never left me hanging in cyberspace. He is professional in every sense, giving sound advice and feedback each step of the way. He and his charming wife Brenda have attended my book launches. I felt very honoured to look out at those assembled and see their smiling faces.

My son went on to write a book about his autism, and his manuscript was accepted and eventually published by GP. It takes great courage to publish writing that sits outside the mainstream. There are risks involved at every turn, but the end result is nothing short of triumphant. For a human being to have their gifts and capacities acknowledged in this way is life-changing indeed.

I have been fortunate to have this wonderful relationship with my publisher. He feels like part of my family. His quiet, unassuming nature is not a true indication of the razor-sharp intellect within. His vision to promote good Australian writers lies at the heart of all he does. In 2003, Stephen received a Centenary Medal for his 'contribution to the writing community and ongoing support for local authors'. In 1997 he won a Canberra Critics Circle Award for Literature for his 'tireless contribution to the writing community'. This speaks to selflessness and dedication.

GP actively cultivates an environment for their writers to link up with each other by being invited to speak at specific events. I participated in such an event after the launching of one of my books. Brenda and Stephen organised a panel of GP poets to speak on the topic Are You Brave Enough to be a Poet?

The authors spoke, and then a lively debate ensued, where ideas were discussed and shared with the audience. It was very much enjoyed by those who participated.

Invited guests and friends were able to understand and learn more about a writer's method and style; how they develop their craft. It also gave those who had taken the time to attend the book launch a real sense of inclusion. Some of the audience asked very pertinent questions, and as a result, the authors had to think carefully about their responses. A great mental workout!

I have a good relationship with other GP writers, especially some of those living in Tasmania. Sometimes we meet up at writers' events, or at book launches, or find each other in the oddest of places. I recently saw a fellow GP poet at the airport, and we managed to have a decent conversation in spite of arrivals and departures. Another GP writing friend lives in Hobart, and we correspond a few times a year. On one occasion, while visiting Hobart, we met up for a coffee, and spoke at length about our writing, and about what motivates and spurs us onwards.

It's very satisfying to spend time with a fellow writer, to experience some soul-searching and connectedness, and to feel totally comfortable with it. It helps reaffirm what we do, and why we do it. It motivates us, and re-energises the passion for our craft. It helps with the isolation of writing; the long hours of solitude and separation from the world.

For this is an irrefutable fact: writing is a solo act. We do it alone, with very little encouragement or appreciation. Many people don't often understand the fervour involved, and see writing as some sort of half-baked hobby. I find this attitude so lacking in empathy, it makes me want to cry.

Do I have a writing career? This is a difficult question to answer. In as much as my goal of being published has been achieved, and in relation to the constraints and obligations of my life, I don't so much see my writing as a career, but as a vocation.

I never sit to write with the intention of make a living from it. I understand how hard it is to do this. Maybe in the halcyon days of another era, and if one had an income stream providing an independent salary of sorts, it could be possible. For a woman, it is even more difficult. The major difficulty is how the rest of the world perceives her.

In many countries of the world, she is born into a certain role, and by the very nature of her sex, seen as a nurturer or care-giver. This mould is a hard one to break free from. Not all women have the same prospects to acquiring an education and literacy. Not all women have the money to buy paper and pens. The world does not stop to allow women to write uninterrupted, free of domesticity and everyday duties. As an Australian woman, I am fortunate.

I seize opportunities to catch segments of time in my life to create my wordscapes. For this is exactly what they are: thoughts born out of reflection, finely honed into visual images formed by the written word. The words are like stones across a river, where each step carries the reader forward, until they reach landfall on the other side.

Maybe it is in this place my reader can rest upon green banks by a river's edge, cloud-gazing or contemplating a world of words constructed for them out of every human emotion and longing. Sometimes it is a place of fear and darkness and suffering, but when it is pure sweetness and light, and a tribute to all things beautiful, I hope the reader finds a sanctuary; a sense of connection. As a poet, I can possess no greater happiness or fulfilment than in being the vessel from which these deepest feelings can pour.

I am a poet published by Ginninderra Press. For this, I am grateful. I hope the literary legacy of my time and place in Australian society, and of my travels into other places on our wonderful planet Earth, can be shared with all those who read my poems. It is the most I can hope for, and lies at the essence of everything I wish to accomplish as a writer; a gift to my readers and an act of love.

Stepping Stones

Bill Cotter

Victorian short story writer and poet

To me, nature, in all its forms, has great therapeutic power. And if, in my poetry, I have conveyed something of that to anyone else, I will be happy.

Whether one writes for one's private pleasure, a few select friends, or for a wider audience, writing will always remain quite an isolated – and potentially an isolating – experience. And, for those seeking a wider readership, there will always remain the problem of finding a publisher.

There are, certainly in Australia and overseas, quite a number of journals and literary magazines that will consider unsolicited work. However, some may have quite an ephemeral existence, and always the competition for acceptance is quite intense. Understandably, journals can only accept a certain number of submissions and, while rejection will always remain a reality, we owe these periodicals a real sense of gratitude. Without their support, little of what we write would, perhaps, ever see the light of day. Certainly, acceptance gives a writer a sense of confidence that his or her writing has not been a waste of time.

If finding acceptance in journals and literary magazines is difficult, one can easily imagine the problems presented if one wants to discover a publisher willing to consider a whole collection. It is a sad observation, but probably a true one, that the readership of poetry in Australia is quite small. So a publisher can, in all likelihood, expect only a small return for their financial outlay.

The reluctance of large publishers to venture into poetry is not difficult to understand. Nor the fact that there are few opportunities for poets to see their work, as a collection, in print. So the value of small, independent publishers is, for a poet, considerable.

How fortunate, therefore, to find, in the 1998 edition of *Australian Writer's Marketplace*, mention of Ginninderra Press (GP), at that time based in Canberra and apparently happy to consider manuscripts of poetry. Perhaps there will always be an element of luck in writing, as, I expect, in other creative ventures, and my good luck was to come across this entry. GP looked, to me, like a potential oasis bobbing up in the barren landscape of publishing. So I sent off a brief résumé of my time as a writer, with mention of work that had been published, and a collection of about 50 poems. Stephen Matthews accepted these, and my first collection, *The Darkness of Swans*, was published by GP in 1999.

Since then, Stephen has published six collections of my poetry. *The White Blood of Moonlight* appeared in 2002, *Cloud Gazing* in 2005, *Refractions* in 2008, *Light Within the Stone* in 2011, *Pen Points* in 2013 and *Of Light, Shade and Half-Light* in 2014.

The last two I actually wrote in calligraphy, with simple (I say very simple) illustrations. It was a challenge for me as the writer. Indeed, I spent hundreds of hours over the task, hours fraught with many mistakes, corrections, rejected pages and amendments. But from it all came a very real admiration for those medieval scribes and illuminators who worked, often under very difficult conditions, to produce works of extraordinary power and beauty. Their depth and beauty remain a source of wonder for people today, particularly for those, like me, who have ventured into the areas of calligraphy and illumination. My own work pales into insignificance when set against those manuscripts.

However, I was most grateful that Stephen, in spite of the technical difficulties, went ahead and published both books for me. The second collection received a very warm review in the literary journal *Tamba*, a tribute probably more to GP's presentation than to my poetry and artwork.

Almost all of my poetry comes from my own experiences. Childhood, I suppose, will always be a resource for expression and personal exploration, and I have mined my own childhood and adolescence for ideas. It is interesting, when looking back over what has been published by GP, to see the importance my father had in my development as a person. I suspect that many sons can make the same observation about their fathers. Whether women have the same response to their mothers I do not know. Such reflective writing also gives one the chance to examine the significance of experiences at a particular moment in one's life.

I live in a very beautiful area of Victoria and I have written a good deal about my relationship with the various landscapes here. Also, I am attracted to deserts and barren areas of the continent.

To me, nature, in all its forms, has great therapeutic power. And if, in my poetry, I have conveyed something of that to anyone else, I will be happy. I do not think, however, that we should see the natural world through rose-tinted glasses. To appreciate the full extent of its power, we need to report it as it is. The environment is not Utopia. I think also that, in order to be honest, we need to actually do some basic research into the aspects we are writing about. Learning about the natural world can be an exciting experience anyway. Indeed, often, while researching and exploring, the actual direction of a piece of writing may change completely. Such is the element of surprise inherent in the world around us.

Stephen has encouraged my interest in the natural world and the fact that poetry can explore the therapeutic relationship we can have with the natural environment.

I have experimented with traditional forms of poetry and free verse. Using the traditional forms has always been a challenge to me, I think because of their insistence on compression and discipline. Sonnets, villanelles, pantoums and ballades can be both frustrating and rewarding. GP has published many of my poems written in traditional forms. This has been most supportive, particularly at a time when, I feel, many publishers, and perhaps many writers as well, are more attracted to free verse.

Stephen also published a short play for voices, *Of Baiame and a Tree That Said, 'Dig'*. This followed the tragic journey of Burke and Wills north to the Gulf of Carpentaria. As I have suggested, the desert areas of Australia have always held a fascination for me and the epic attempt by Burke and Wills to be the first to cross the continent from south to north and back again gave me the opportunity to write something different: a play in verse written to be heard rather than presented on stage. It was my good fortune that, in 2001, Stephen began to publish some works of drama. I am sure that, had he not agreed to take on my short play, it would not have appeared in print.

GP has also published a collection of my short stories. Most of those, too, were a reflection on my experiences as a younger person or as a teacher in schools in Victoria.

I have had a long association with GP and I am delighted to be able to express my gratitude for Stephen's encouragement over those years. I have appreciated his professional approach and his commitment to producing books of high quality.

I must express my admiration, too, for Stephen's innovative approach to publishing. The Pocket Poets series has broken new ground and I know that he is also producing pocket chapbooks on significant places and people.

Although my wife Kay and I live in Bairnsdale, a long way from Adelaide, Stephen has come to all but one of my book launches and that, for a writer, is much appreciated.

We have been able to attend a number of literary events in Canberra and Adelaide. I mentioned earlier that writing can be quite a lonely activity, particularly when one is far from the cultural centres one finds in larger cities. These events give writers from different backgrounds and interests the chance to come together and share ideas. Such events will always be valuable for writers. They also demonstrate Stephen's commitment to furthering the wider community's appreciation of literature and its place within society. Clearly, too, these gatherings give writers the chance to be seen and heard by a wider audience.

It is true for me, and probably true for many other GP writers as well, that being published opens a number of doors within a community. I have been able to conduct writing courses for adults and children, judge competitions and take part in public readings, largely because people know that a reputable publisher has promoted my work.

I would like to make one further observation about the relationship between writers and publishers. Or, rather, one that demonstrates the central importance publishers have for the creative development of writers. Some time ago, I ran a number of writing activities for primary school children in Bairnsdale. The students were very open and enthusiastic, and at one point I asked them why they wrote. Two of them said that when they were angry or depressed they would go to their rooms and write down their feelings. These children would know nothing at all about the therapeutic value of art. Yet they were bearing testimony to it. So what I suggested earlier about the personal value of nature poetry has a much wider significance. A significance for a writer that Stephen, as a publisher, has recognised.

Finally, I would like to express my appreciation for Stephen's friendship over a long period. This has made the whole experience of writing for publication a most enjoyable one. I am delighted, in saying this, to express my pleasure that GP has recently expanded its business.

I know that, in recent years, Brenda, Stephen's wife, herself a writer, has become an integral part of the business. I include her in these remarks as well. She has always been most encouraging about my work. And I know that, given the expansion of GP, her participation has become increasingly important.

Without the support of Stephen and Brenda, my writing would not have received the public exposure it has. Certainly my involvement with them has given a focus to many of my endeavours.

Recently, Stephen suggested that I might put together a collection of poetry that I have written over the past 30 years or so. I was delighted to do this and *Mirror: New & selected poems* has been published this year.

Stephen is a very unassuming person. However, his pleasant, optimistic approach has, I am sure, been appreciated by all those who have been published by GP. The medal he received for his service to the literary community in Canberra showed that his work was valued greatly in that city.

I am very happy to express my gratitude here, knowing that there are many other writers throughout Australia who share those feelings.

And, with everyone else, I extend my congratulations. Twenty years of continual publishing in Australia is certainly a reason for celebration. I am proud to have had such a long association with Ginninderra Press.

From the Darkness to the Light

Brenda Eldridge

South Australian poet, non-fiction writer and editor

I can remember so clearly literally dancing on the pavement when I took the first copy of my book out of my mail box. My dream had come true! I was a published poet!

I began writing in 1986 as therapy to deal with the harsher realities of life. My dad had died and suddenly I felt I had been cast adrift in the universe – the severing of the silver cord between us. I had not seen or spoken to him since 1970, when I left England to start a new life in Australia with my husband and young sons. The silence was only due to the limitations of access to phones in those far-off days. I wrote about my childhood growing up in a small English village to remind myself who I was, and this proved vital in the following years.

My marriage had disintegrated and in 1991 one of my sons took his own life. I found once again that writing enabled me to rebuild myself. This time it was poetry that saved me, strengthening my connection with nature and the resilience of life lusting after life. I discovered that, once started, I was a compulsive writer. Nothing has changed in that respect, as I have drifted between poetry and non-fiction prose.

In those very dark times, I felt as if every dream I had was shattered. The gods, it seemed, had other ideas. One lunchtime in 1995, while walking beside a chuckling stream under the trees near where I worked, a friend asked if I had a dream of my own. My answer was instant: 'I want to be a published poet.' I was startled, not only by the quickness of my response, but by how fiercely I felt it. This was something I wanted for myself and had nothing to do with friends or family. For it to come true was dependent on a publisher who would see something in my words, worthy of being sent out in the vast public domain.

In 2003 I collated almost 200 poems from among the many hundreds I had written and took them to a local printer/binding shop that relieved me of my money and returned them to me as two nicely bound volumes with spiral backs and mock-leather cardboard covers. I took them home, put them on a shelf and they stayed there untouched for five years.

In 2008 a friend called in to take me out for a meal and, not being quite ready, I gave him one of my volumes to read. His response to the poems was to ask if he could take them and try and find a publisher for them. Well, that was more than I had courage for, so I was happy to leave them in his hands.

Weeks went by, so I was taken completely by surprise when my friend told me he had found Ginninderra Press (GP) and that I had an appointment with Stephen Matthews. I didn't know how unusual this was for Stephen, who I learned from experience is reclusive by nature but also has to be strict with his time. If he spent as much time talking with his writers as most of us would like, the publishing would not get done at all. I didn't really know what I was supposed to do or say. Stephen said he would publish some of my poetry. I was so astonished that, when he asked me if I had any questions, I could only think to ask how to pronounce 'ginninderra'.

A few months later in early 2009, my book *The Silver Cord* was ready – but not without the briefest of tussles over the title. Needless to say, Stephen had his way. I can remember so clearly literally dancing on the pavement when I took the first copy out of my mail box. My dream had come true! I was a published poet!

When I went to pick up some books from Stephen to hopefully sell to work colleagues, he asked me about a launch for my book. Launch! I hadn't thought beyond being published. Stephen also casually said, 'I'm going out on a limb here. Would you like to go out to dinner?'

Stephen had not long moved from Canberra to South Australia when I first met him in 2008. Some time before I knew he existed, I had decided I wanted a complete change to the way I was living. Serendipity or the gods, here were two people looking to make a new start in life. Stephen and I caused a bit of a stir among our families when we decided in May 2009, after only knowing each other for a very short time, that we wanted to live together. And so began another new life.

Now, I am the first one to admit this sequence of events doesn't happen to every poet with the dream of becoming published, but I have also openly admitted, becoming a published poet turned my life inside out and upside down. *The Silver Cord* was vindication of me as a poet. This was my dream and it had come true. Nothing could change or damage that. *The Silver Cord* was launched as part of a panel discussion on the theme of Writing from the Dark with Zenda Vecchio and Ken Vincent at the Tea Tree Gully Library. For the first time in my life, I was with like-minded people – fellow writers who became very dear friends. And I have gone on to form other close relationships with other writers. We are the GP family.

So what is it like living with a publisher?

Well, from my personal point of view, it is magic. I have seen more of Australia in our time together than I had in the previous 30-something years, as we travel the country to attend book launches. I love book launches. For a writer, there can be few things sweeter than sitting at a table signing copies of your book which someone has just bought. Now that is the stuff of dreams.

I recall at the same time Stephen had his run-in with cancer in 2010, he published a book about an author's experiences with breast cancer. I don't know how Stephen managed to do that. I was cowardly and didn't even read it, but things have a way of making us do what is right. As it turned out, the lady who was supposed to launch the book suddenly found she was battling breast cancer too, and I was asked to step in to do the launch. Obviously, I had to read the book, and I am so glad I did, because it gave me yet another insight into the nightmare that touches the lives of anyone taking on this insidious monster – cancer. I had written poetry daily during the time Stephen was in hospital and in the weeks he was undergoing radiotherapy treatment, but that was from my perspective as the onlooker. To my surprise, Stephen published some of my poems in a book entitled *Facing Cancer*; I could not imagine what he was going through.

We have been made welcome at so many different venues but when it comes to libraries, Tea Tree Gully, in the north-east suburbs of Adelaide, has to be the best. The enthusiastic support we and local writers have received from the staff there has been nothing short of wonderful. They provide us with a beautiful space for book launches and panel events, plus tea, coffee, wine and nibbles. I must confess that it was my desire to have my collection *Tangled Roots: New and selected poems*, launched there for my 65th birthday because the library presented me, as it does with other authors, a bottle of wine with the book's cover image on the label. This makes a special occasion all the more precious.

My favourite venue for book launches and literary events is East Avenue Books in Clarence Park. This is the quintessential second-hand bookshop, with polished wooden floors, timber bookcases and treasures locked in a glass-fronted cabinet. The owners, Peter and Joan, couldn't have been more supportive and welcoming. Peter makes a great master of ceremonies. We have had gatherings where just a few people have turned up and other times when we could barely fit everyone in, but the atmosphere is always everything I ever dreamed of. My only complaint is that I never seem to leave the shop without buying a book – or two or three… I have said for many, many years, my last dollar will always be spent on a book!

All the travelling and book launches make life exciting but they are the external bonuses of living with a publisher. We have another, quieter life where we live down by the tidal reach.

Stephen has been a one-man band as GP since 1996, before coming to Port Adelaide alone in 2008. In February 2010, I retired after 25 years working for Centrelink. It took several months of doing nothing with my days, beyond enjoying life with Stephen, before I felt ready to take on something new. I had already become part of the gentle routine of Stephen's life, like going to the post office at 9 a.m. to collect the mail. I love to find cards in the mail box that mean there are packages inside to be collected, because I had learned that these packages were usually manuscripts from hopeful writers.

Once home, Stephen registers the arrival of each package in the computer and places the manuscripts in his in-tray to be read. A clarification of 'in-tray' is significant. Our sitting room is a large square room with the kitchen in one corner opposite the floor-to-ceiling windows and French doors that form the front of the room overlooking the tidal reach. Between the kitchen area and the windows is 'the cosy corner' – so named because of the soft lounge suite that sits in there, arranged to separate it from the rest of the space. Like any home with this set-up, we have a coffee table with a shelf underneath – and this shelf is Stephen's in-tray. Manuscripts have to sit there patiently until once a month or so he takes them all out – usually on a weekend – to see what delights await him.

In the early days, I speculated about what Stephen looked for in a manuscript and could only come up with 'It has to be something that makes him go "Ah".' Probably not helpful to hopeful writers. When I first retired, I loved to look through the manuscripts and have a sneaky read. I certainly felt honoured when Stephen asked me to read something he was hesitant about accepting.

But my role was to change drastically. Oh! Before I go any further, I think I should say that the heart of GP is Stephen's office just inside the front door. This is where two computers and three printers and other assorted machines have produced hundreds of books (the thermal-bound ones and the stapled chapbooks). I have to say it was really weird when we first moved in together to go downstairs in the dark, in the middle of the night, and be faced by all the different stand-by lights. It looked a bit like a fairy grotto. Meanwhile, my studio is upstairs overlooking the tidal reach. Probably the least said about this the better as I spend many hours in my studio not just working for GP, but writing and painting…and gazing out of the window at dolphins, and pelicans and other assorted birds.

Stephen showed me how to take the electronic copy of a manuscript he had accepted and do the initial lay-out and preparation to turn it into a book. When I think of the hours writers spend in typing up their words, choosing just the right font and its size, line spacing, the use of capital letters and italics and so on, it makes me shudder, as there are GP fixed elements and house styles. So I don't think about those aspects any more than I can help. In my early days doing this, I loved the manuscripts that had to be scanned or that came through on older-style computers. The text was all mixed up with odd symbols and wingdings – such fun to delete the extraneous bits and really get to know the actual poetry.

This means I read everything at least twice, as I convert the text to the GP font and spacing styles, seek out spelling, grammar and punctuation errors (rest assured, all writers – Stephen checks all this when he gets it back). Sometimes I think the space bar, the ellipsis and the exclamation mark should be abolished from keyboards. Stephen says he isn't a writer but he is an expert reader. That needs some thinking about. He has gradually taught me that a lot of extra aids to the reader are not needed and writers should have more faith in their reader's ability to understand what they are saying.

It's the same with the order poems are placed in a collection. I have done this – spent hours putting poems in what I think is the correct order – only to learn over time that people will most likely randomly open pages, or pick something by its title rather than read from cover to cover. It made a big difference to me once I managed to get my head around it.

Back to the preparation work. To help me in what I do Stephen has given me my own 'bible', *The New Oxford Dictionary for Writers and Editors*. It is a brilliant book that tells me when something should be italicised or capitalised or where points go with abbreviations. I'm not good at spelling and I have the *Macquarie ABC Dictionary* on my desk and use it often. The secret is, of course, knowing when something is misspelt and if you don't…well, this has been known to produce a sort of 'tsk' from the boss! It is rewarding to feel as though I am taking an active part in the publication of books.

Stephen is publishing fewer novels since his experience with cancer. In the days he lay in the hospital, he re-evaluated a lot of things in his life, and decided that novels were very labour-intensive and time-consuming. He still does publish a few for authors whose work he has published before.

Non-fiction as a genre is always full of surprises. In my preparation work, I have read about things that I would never have done otherwise: topics such as how Canberra was developed; the lives of migrants; the stories of people struggling with Down syndrome, autism, or dyslexia. The latter was a revelation because at the time the author was growing up, dyslexia wasn't even in the dictionary!

In my life, I haven't read a vast amount of poetry. On consideration, I believe this to be a good thing. It meant when I started writing my own, I wasn't influenced by the established poets. Hmm. Honesty demands that I can happily acknowledge that Kate Llewellyn was an influence. I read her *Dear You* in the 90s and loved her style of prose and poetry – and her way of life in Leura. However, I did know I didn't like the style of the Australian greats like Paterson or Lawson. Why? Too many words. I prefer to read as I write; using a few, well chosen words that provide a framework that the reader can fill in for themselves with a bit of quiet contemplation. It's about writing to make people think rather than feeding them a prepared meal.

Working with Stephen has meant that I now read a lot of poetry. It doesn't matter whether I like a collection or not, because Stephen as Mr GP has already made the decision to publish it. I am often puzzled as to what he has seen that I have missed and this certainly makes me read poetry differently.

In mid-2014, serendipity was obviously at work again. A GP author in Victoria and another in South Australia, in the same week, and unknown to each other, both asked Stephen about having a chapbook. Stephen had been pondering over chapbooks for some time, but other than knowing he didn't want to replicate the old standard format for them, nothing had happened. So here it was – a new challenge. Those ponderings came to the surface and he first declared the chapbooks were going to be a different size. It was more practical to have them the size of a business envelope, as this meant they could fit into a handbag or pocket – hence, the instant leap to calling them Pocket Poets. Significantly, it also meant posting them was less costly. The next thing was the covers. Again, Stephen wanted to break from tradition, and let the writers choose an image that filled the whole cover and would be in colour. Style was the next thing. It was important to keep the chapbooks in line with other GP publications of poetry, which meant there would be only one poem per page, a maximum of 20 to a chapbook. The final stipulation was that they could only be written by GP authors.

I think we were both astounded by the instant success of the Pocket Poets. We found some of our authors wanted to use them instead of greeting cards, or as a small gift, for the fast approaching Christmas season. We sold 1,200 chapbooks in about three months. As of May 2016, there were over 45 titles in the series.

Good ideas come from hidden depths and have been initiated by chance remarks. Over lunch one day, at the beginning of 2015, someone made such a chance remark, and before long we had the idea of chapbooks for prose: Pocket Polemics, Pocket People and Pocket Places. I did wonder if the Pocket Polemics would take the place of *Voice* magazine, which had only finished a couple of years earlier. Five thousand words to write about something or someone we feel passionately about is apparently no real hardship, and we are gathering quite a collection of the prose Pockets. In May 2016, there were 20 prose Pockets. Total sales of all the Pocket series were 3,770 copies.

The winds of change had begun to blow through our lives and very soon we were to feel it keenly. In October 2014, someone Stephen knew about 25 years ago in Canberra contacted him out of the blue. Now a representative of Ingram Spark, a multinational printer/distributor, she asked if he would be interested in a new mode of production for GP publications. This was a big decision with many different things to be considered. Stephen is very conscious of how hard survival is for a small business. If he embraced this new idea, then one of the casualties would be the orders placed with the small, local printing firm who had done such a wonderful job with many GP books since Stephen moved to Adelaide. For years, GP had also produced thermal-bound books for those authors who could not afford a conventional print run. These were printed on demand and made in-house. Spark was offering print on demand at affordable prices and worldwide distribution, which included ebook versions and a presence on websites such as Amazon and Book Depository. This meant that thermal-bound books were discontinued.

Stephen put my collection of five non-fiction books (*Down by the River*, *It's Still Out There*, *Tales From My Patagonia*, *There's a Rainbow Serpent in My Garden* and *Eastwards*) into one volume entitled *From Patagonia to Australia* and had it printed by Spark to see what quality we could expect. We were delighted by the result. The decision was made and GP publications now have a very distinctive appearance and feel.

But serendipity was not over for GP. Some would say it was by chance, but I prefer to think the gods were watching over us. In March 2015, while checking Facebook, Stephen came across a post that Picaro Press was looking for a new owner. Within a week, Stephen had taken over Picaro Press.

I think it is fair to say that our lives, since the takeover, have changed a lot. Unbeknownst to me, Stephen had been thinking of winding the business down a bit before the Pocket Poets idea emerged. Instead, one way or another, we have become busier than ever. We have laughingly called Stephen a media mogul but there was a serious side to this. Stephen inherited a stable of many authors. Would they want their publications reprinted under the GP imprint? What would happen to the chapbooks?

What an amazing opportunity this turned out to be for me. There was a flood of emotions when Stephen asked me to be Mrs Editor of the chapbook series that was to be known as Picaro Poets. I was flattered, honoured and, quite frankly, scared by this show of faith in my abilities.

The Picaro Poets chapbooks were to be open to all writers. This meant, for me, no more comfort zone. The Pocket Poets were proven quality GP writers. Now I was the one having to make the decisions about what was going to be published and what wasn't.

What were the Picaro Poets chapbooks going to look like? I confess, I love the traditional style of chapbooks with their parchment covers and the black and white woodcut prints and the vellum sheet between cover and text. I like the size of them too – they really look like a small book! I kept very quiet while Stephen was musing about the new series. All the practical and aesthetic reasons for creating the size of the Pocket Poets were sound, so the new series would follow suit. How to make them distinctive from the Pockets? Yes! They have parchment covers and the vellum sheet. Cover image? The gentle art of compromise here. An image that measures about eight centimetres square and is printed in greyscale. The last differences – there were to be 24 pages for text and they would cost $5 each, not the $4 of the Pockets.

Stephen almost casually asked if I could give him 24 poems so we could make a sample volume. This wasn't the first time I have been a GP guinea pig and I really didn't mind.

We had the formal launch of the Picaro Poet series of chapbooks at East Avenue Books in September 2015. At that time, we had 11 titles on the GP website; there are now almost 30.

It wasn't until I came to write my speech for the launch event that I realised how important the chapbooks are to writers daring themselves to send in poetry to a publisher. I think I could have tried getting a few poems published in a chapbook if I had known about them all those years ago when I left my manuscript languishing on the shelf. Much easier to risk 20 or so poems being rejected than 50 or more.

I have learned that I can read just a few poems in a submission and know whether I am going to say yes or no. When in doubt, Stephen has been wonderfully supportive. Anyone who knows Stephen knows he is a man of few words. I asked him to read a submission I was in doubt about. His answer? 'Tosh.' I had also had a glimpse by then of the impact I was having as Mrs Editor saying yes to a collection of poetry. These poets, some who had never had anything published before anywhere, were as overwhelmed as I had been when Stephen accepted my poetry for *The Silver Cord*. I am, in effect, paying it forward. It is the most extraordinary feeling.

With all the clever advances in modern technology, doubt has been cast about the future of printed books. It is a sad fact that many bookshops have not survived the trend towards ebooks or big publishing houses flooding supermarkets and newsagents with cheap books, and of course the availability of books via the Internet. But I only have to look at the manuscripts waiting to be read in our sitting room, or the list in our computers of titles in the process of becoming books, to know that books will be in demand as long as there are writers.

Who knows, maybe it will all go back to scratchings on wax tablets, or symbols on papyrus, but one thing is for sure, nothing lasts forever, not the good things or the bad, and everything moves in cycles. I am just so happy I am living in the age of printed books and that I am sharing my life with the independent publisher Stephen Matthews.

Finding a Voice

Ian McFarlane

New South Wales novelist, essayist, critic and poet

> I've always passionately believed in the possibility of a fully engaged community, where access to marginalised regions of cultural connection, such as poetry, would be open and available to everyone, rather than tightly controlled by a few gatekeepers, too often concerned with showing each other how clever they are.

I first met Stephen Matthews in 1992 when trying to slip unnoticed into Canberra's ANU bookshop to see if my third novel, *Shadows*, recently published by Hale & Iremonger and receiving excellent reviews, was adequately displayed. Happily, it was, as Stephen – who was then managing the bookshop – obligingly pointed out. I'm usually disinclined, socially and psychologically, to engage in conversation with people I have never previously met, but we slipped easily into an exchange of views on books and writing, and it soon became clear that Stephen's knowledge and opinions were quietly professional, as well as being shaped by a genuine love of literature. Leaving the bookshop, I was somehow sure our paths would cross again.

And of course they did, leading to a much-valued friendship, based on similar attitudes to many things, such as the role of literature in reaching a truly civilised and environmentally sustainable society, and later, a long-standing professional association, based on my becoming a Ginninderra Press author, and then part of the editorial team involved with the production of *Voice*, a quarterly journal of comment and review, dedicated to ideas, especially those from outside the established hierarchy.

For me, this last point is a core issue. I've always passionately believed in the possibility of a fully engaged community, where access to marginalised regions of cultural connection, such as poetry, would be open and available to everyone, rather than tightly controlled by a few gatekeepers, too often concerned with showing each other how clever they are. And my Ginninderra Press (GP) essays and poems reflect this personal crusade, often to my detriment. Take, for example, my 2014 GP collection of poetry, *The Shapes of Light*, which included an elegant introduction

by Stephen, and a preface based on one of my essays published in *The Australian Literary Review*. This received a disingenuously snide backhander from a leading Oz poetry insider, seemingly based on a couple of poems satirising wilful obscurity (among a total of well over 100 poems on many other things), and despite being successfully launched at the 2014 Penola Arts Festival in South Australia, where I had been invited as result of a long-held admiration for the lyric verse of John Shaw Neilson. In Penola, I was grateful for the presence of Stephen and Brenda, who kindly took the trouble to drive from Adelaide for the launch by singer/songwriter Darryl Emmerson, who had beautifully arranged several Neilson poems as songs. Darryl's selected readings from *The Shapes of Light* (together with mine) were given warm applause for their audibly poetic cadence and accessibility, which seemed to confirm what I was trying to do with the collection.

However, there is a much more crucially defining aspect to my identity as a writer – the often suffocating darkness of anxiety and clinical depression – which has so deeply scarred my life, it would be difficult, if not impossible, to ignore in the context of my respect and admiration for GP as a vibrant element in the culturally complex mosaic of Australian books and writing. And therefore, it might be useful to widen the narrative lens with a quick charcoal sketch, or a little of what old-stagers might call *mise en scène*.

I have always loved words, and would scribble constantly in childhood notebooks on the south coast of England. At the age of 14, I answered a BBC radio request for poems about a journey's end, heavily borrowing, I suspect, from Robert Louis Stevenson, in composing a cascade of four-line stanzas describing a river winding through valleys and forests before reaching the sea. Carefully folding the bunch of handwritten pages into the biggest envelope I could find, I delivered my epic verse to our friendly postman, and waited for what seemed like an eternity (it was probably only a matter of weeks) until being astonished to receive a letter from the BBC saying my poem had been selected for a broadcast reading.

Two years later, having arrived in Western Australia as part of a large family of 'ten pound Pom' migrants, I edited a migrant hostel news-sheet and wrote, directed and acted in my own play, a swashbuckling warm-up drama for the Hostel Theatrical Society's main performance of a satirical comedy skit on English migrants. With perhaps forgivably mistaken youthful enthusiasm, I imagined my dream of becoming a writer had arrived early, but my first novel, *The Jerusalem Conspiracy*, was not published until many years later, by Rigby in 1984. This was loosely based on notebook jottings gathered during a Foreign Service posting to Israel in the relative calm between the Six Day War of 1968 and the Yom Kippur War of 1973.

I'd previously published short stories and minor essays, but writing this debut novel was also a desperately sought distraction during a painfully long recovery from the nervous breakdown that cut short my Foreign Service career. A second posting, involving the withering stress of too many over-long hours in the crowded confusion of Hong Kong, had presented what seemed – for me, at least – a greater threat to psychological well-being than the routine horror of terrorism and war in Israel. Writing was part of the long road back, harassed along the way by a catalogue of anxiety disorders that defy easy explanation, such as agoraphobia and crippling panic attacks. Even so, I managed to complete a mature age Arts degree, begin what was to become the mainstay of my professional writing – book reviews and essays – while laying down a narrative framework for *The Siberian Sparrows*, followed by what I like to think of as a testimonial work, *Shadows*, both published by Hale & Iremonger, in 1991 and 1992.

As mentioned earlier, *Shadows* provided a serendipitous chance to meet Stephen, and part of this process came about through meeting Bill Tully, a warmly Chaucerian figure of a man, when I agreed to an interview hosted on the ANU's public radio station, 2XX, concerning *The Siberian Sparrows*. Bill was then working at the National Library of Australia, and variously described as a 'Canberra treasure', or – as he preferred to see himself – as a '*flâneur*', which I understood to be a French 'stroller'; a term used by Baudelaire to portray someone inclined to wander a city 'in order to experience it'. Bill suited the role well, strolling the byways of Civic, Canberra's cultural and commercial hub, to browse bookshops and coffee parlours, and occasionally engage friends and bystanders with idiosyncratic opinions on politics, poetry and philosophy.

As a cyber-sceptic of even greater dimension than me, Bill could be hard to contact at short notice in an age hungrily embracing instant communication and the paranoia of right-wing politics. I fondly remember one day when visiting Canberra from the coast with my wife, Mary, and wanting to speak to Bill, suggesting, half playfully, that if we were to loiter in Garema Place for 15 minutes, he would no doubt appear – and sure enough, less than 10 minutes later, Bill flâneured into sight, greeting us warmly, and without surprise, as if it had all been previously arranged.

The Siberian Sparrows was set largely in Canberra, including a scene that takes place in a well-known coffee shop, pioneered by a charismatic immigrant from Vienna, Gus Petersilka, who took great satisfaction in disregarding old-fashioned Australian custom and by-laws by allowing his tables and chairs to spill out over adjacent pavements. Of course, Bill was delighted by this rebellion, and intrigued by the way my novel, a psychological thriller with Petrov connotations, had wandered into one of his favourite cafés, giving a glimpse of how early Canberra, like many Australian cities – in spite of obvious climatic suitability – had been slow to accept a European taste for al fresco dining. For Bill, who was then editing a little lit mag called *Blast*, Gus Petersilka's inventively argumentative coffee shop – which eventually led to some frowsy attitudes regarding street-side coffee undergoing a charmingly multicultural make-over – offered a rich source of creative material.

The Siberian Sparrows implicated persistent rumours that Australian Intelligence had been penetrated by the Russians, and Bill opened my 2XX radio interview by playing the Romance from *The Gadfly* by Shostakovich. This well-known theme also introduced a successful ABC TV drama series, *Reilly, Ace of Spies*, starring Sam Neil, and I was seduced (and gratefully surprised) by how well the music relaxed me. I've somehow retained an intense schoolyard shyness, which has, as an adult, become a willing accomplice to chronic anxiety and clinical depression, but Bill's interview – one of my early public encounters – went very well, no doubt largely due to his comfortably meandering interviewing style, but also because we both believe in social justice and the ways in which books and writing can open dialogues based more on cooperation than competition. When Stephen bravely opened an independent publishing venture (GP) in 1996, with similar inclinations, it was only a matter of time before the three of us would find a shared literary voice with the eponymous quarterly journal of comment and review.

However, all that came later, after tenuously navigating the nervous 90s, with the millennium drawing nigh, amid rumours of digital disaster with the so-called Y2K bug causing havoc if binary computer systems failed to register the year 2000 without frying their chips. There was serious talk of financial meltdown and even of planes falling out of the sky as clocks ticked down on New Year's Eve 1999. In the event, the embarrassing anticlimax of nothing happening fuelled a global hangover of relieved scepticism and coy credulity; dusted off by a few sheepish shrugs from the dithering digerati.

Meanwhile, I was trying to cope with the disappointment of Hale & Iremonger withdrawing from fiction – despite the critical (if not financial) success of my second and third novels – and therefore having to face the mountain of trying to find a home for my nearly completed fourth novel, chapters of which were written in Eleanor Dark's garden studio at Varuna during a three-week residential fellowship in the winter of 1993. Given that I was now an established writer (having had three novels accepted by mainstream publishers), I imagined – perhaps ambitiously and definitely naively – that finding a new mainstream publisher would be no big deal. The trouble is, my fiction writing doesn't slide comfortably into any commercially driven genre, and I've never been good at (or particularly inclined towards) singing and dancing the publicity gigs authors are increasingly required to do, and made the silly mistake of assuming I just needed to turn up. After all, I'd received rave reviews, including (in *The Australian*) praise that suggested I wrote 'like a dream [with] some of the sentences so beautiful the tongue is forced to silently give shape to them'. And for a brief while, it seemed that all would be well, with a leading mainstream publisher showing strong interest in the new manuscript. Sadly, last-minute changes of staff at senior editorial level also led to a change of direction which apparently didn't include my novel (another psychological thriller based on the rise of terrorism in ways that turned out to be spookily authentic) despite having sought and received extremely positive readers' reports. When similar bad luck was repeated from at least two more leading-name publishers, I shoved the novel into a proverbial bottom drawer, where – from a combination of disappointment and depression-induced writer's block – it remains to this day; hidden from sight, although still containing what one editor described as 'passages of luminous beauty'.

I've always believed the best way to learn to write is to write, and keep writing, until reaching the singular point of self-knowledge that allows recognition of the crucially important difference between wanting and needing to write. I understand the lonely sweat of creative writing as well as anyone, but the risibly insidious cult of celebrity authorship must be resisted. Authorship is earned, never assumed. And there's a damn sight more to being a writer than simply wanting to be one.

Sadly, my life following *Shadows* soon darkened into a wilderness of monochrome monotony, where days slithered into weeks, weeks into months, and months into years; all curiously lacking colour, like sepia-toned and flickering images from a tediously repeated slide show loop. Despite a loving wife and supportive family, it seemed like I had been sent into exile without leaving home. In fact, I was seriously depressed. Clinical depression is an acutely complicated illness, unforgivably individual, and often unreachable to outsiders, even family and close friends. The sense of isolation became so intense; it felt as if I really was the quick charcoal sketch, being slowly and irretrievably erased into the oblivion of a blank sheet of white page. I developed an ability to disguise this despair, with convincing nods and smiles in appropriate directions at social or professional gatherings, but the sheer exhaustion caused by these deceptions left me emotionally and physically spent, and weary beyond imagining. Following another visit to a psychiatric ward with intensive counselling, I began – more in desperation than creativity – to write about how the experience of depression felt, in fiction, prose and verse, with a collection of stories, essays and poems, titled *Evening at Murunna Point*, which Stephen later helped into print with GP in 2001.

Nowadays, everyone seems to be writing about depression (I reviewed at least half a dozen books on the subject in as many years) and it's easy to forget that not so long ago, the black dog was still a strictly taboo subject. The 2001 Canberra launch of *Evening at Murunna Point* is therefore one of my most treasured GP memories. I was part of a panel discussion, including a couple of other GP writers and a psychiatrist, followed by questions from the audience. It was an extraordinary experience: liberating; vividly insightful, and at times deeply affecting. I am profoundly grateful for Stephen's empathy in facilitating this event.

Another GP launch I like to remember (although for different reasons) took place on a rainy Canberra evening in March 2002, when Stephen, Bill and I listened to the then editor of *The Canberra Times*, speaking in a bookshop that no longer exists as he introduced *Voice*; basically, another 'little lit mag' at a time when such a venture might have been described by Sir Humphrey, from the exquisitely (and often hilariously) accurate bureaucratic comedy *Yes, Minister*, as 'a courageous decision', implying, of course, that it was doomed. In fact, *Voice* lasted 11 years in print form, making a wonderfully eclectic (if probably under-appreciated) contribution to Australian ideas, and is certainly worth remembering, particularly in the context of the 20th anniversary of GP as a small, independent publishing outlet in a literary system heavily mortgaged to mainstream marketing.

And since our purpose here is to acknowledge and celebrate cultural contributions, it might be useful to attempt a few definitions: language is the scaffolding of literature; literature is the interpretation of culture; and culture is an expression of collective meaning. And collective meaning is the living, breathing core of humanity: the beginning and the end of everything. At least, as far as us wretched creatures are concerned. The act of choosing a good book, turning its pages, and entering its imagination, with an open mind, is just one step on the long journey towards a truly civilised reality. And a good book – in other words, one that reasonably might be considered as literature – is likely to be a book that uses language with honesty and elegance; elegance with substance; and substance with intelligence. All of which can be linked to the social empathy and grass roots inclusion philosophy of GP.

Of course, such loaded statements invite thinking, but the trouble with thinking is how quickly it becomes a dangerous occupation. Think about it. Philosophy says we need to think in order to validate existence, while psychology reminds us that the process of thinking is constantly challenged by doubt if done honestly, distorted by ignorance if handled superficially, or inflated by hubris if allowed to become too self-absorbed. And, if all that isn't bad enough, it's usually the thinkers who get rounded up and silenced when society breaks down. There's an ineffably profound (and curiously depressing) irony in the way thinking about thinking – as philosophy and psychology must do in order to function – will inevitably lean more towards revealing darker shadows than shedding new light. Shakespeare tells us 'there is nothing either good or bad, but thinking makes it so', and the frequently prejudiced and irrational nonsense used to justify some of our less attractive human behaviour, based on intolerance, cruelty and war, bears witness to the accuracy of such a thought. Personally, I've always been attracted to the arts (and writing is probably one of the most difficult and almost certainly the most subjective) as a search for meaning in a godless universe, but the toxic legacy of a couple of nervous breakdowns would seem to suggest that over-egging a search for truth can be counter-intuitive as well as counter-productive.

Frankly, it has taken me far too long to realise that most of my life problems; certainly those related to the tragically endless loop between anxiety and depression, are crucially linked to over-thinking. Thinking is useful, but too much can be harmful. I guess an analogy might be made with the perfectly poached egg, which requires a calm but inquisitive heat, with a narrow window of opportunity for success. Finishing too early leaves an excessively fluid yolk, while pressing on too long delivers a rubbery yellow ball. The perfectly poached egg – not too runny and not too hard – involves a sequence of optimistic failures in search of pessimistic success, rather like writing a Sufi poem. In short, there's a mystical dimension; irretrievably imprisoned by the hopeless impossibility of our constant search for infinite answers to finite questions. However, since I don't believe in God, I have no use of prayer, although the logical purity of what is commonly known as the serenity prayer has seductive power: 'Please grant me the serenity to accept the things I cannot change; the courage to change the things I can, and the wisdom to know the difference.' In a cynical world of digital distraction and pop psychology, this kind of simple wisdom might be easy to disparage – but it's also difficult to dispute.

I guess the simple (perhaps childlike) truth with which I have always regarded literature and, in particular, poetry, is that – stripped of academic overtone and deconstructive double-speak – there's a dimension for which there are no text-based algorithms; merely honest application in striving to reach Wordsworth's 'still, sad music of humanity'.

When speaking briefly at the launch of *Voice*, I remember noting that despite access to the (at least) 6,000 languages our human species had invented since the dawn of recorded time, we still hadn't managed to speak to each other in a manner entirely free of patronage, prejudice or persecution. It was a *Voice* custom, particularly in the early years, to hold public forums that coincided with the release of a new issue, and invite speakers to reflect on topics, ranging from refugees, literature and indigenous affairs to many others. Our print contributors spanned ages from 18 to 80, with opinions from public intellectualism to everyday common sense, and I take some pride in our public forum in Bermagui, where we filled the community hall with an audience of over 200 people to hear a panel comprising the talented –

but sadly under-used – federal Labor politician Carmen Lawrence, successful author Rosie Scott, and two brightly articulate local high school students (one male, one female) speak about environmental sustainability before inviting questions and discussion from the floor. It is moments like this – I remember thinking at the time, and writing about afterwards – that seem to catch the essence of social relevance and literary democracy, with its tantalisingly possibilities of helping to secure a credible future for a better world. And this, I suggest in closing, aptly summarises the ethos of Stephen and Brenda's Ginninderra Press. I offer my congratulations, and wish them well for the future.

Sincerely Speaking

Maureen Mitson

South Australian historical novelist, short story writer and poet

> 'Mrs Mitson! I read your book. History really happened, didn't it?'
> I was elated.

It was a grey and drizzly English day in October 2008. I was searching for the grave of my maternal grandmother. Its site I had located online, back home in Adelaide – this was the municipal cemetery, a weighty title. I'd been given a number to find. It was somewhere among these acres of overgrown grass; a number, her ID for almost 70 years. It was virtually all I knew of her; my mother's Scots mother who died when my mum was only a girl. Her father and relatives were all in a Scottish churchyard; it seemed wrong that she should be buried in an English cemetery, and alone.

Musing on fate while trudging along, I tripped and nearly over-balanced as my toe struck a weathered bronze plaque. There was lettering; it was barely decipherable but I could read her name: Mary Peach neé Kerr. I had found her: my mother's mother, who could not have anticipated the six grandchildren, 11 great-grandchildren and numerous great-great-grandchildren who were her direct bloodline descendants; Australians all. I was her eldest grandchild. I felt it was my responsibility to learn as much as possible about her and make her part of the large family on the other side of the world that came about only because of her. She would be unearthed. Literally, and by me.

It took about three years of worldwide investigative research, its recording and writing. What piqued my interest and proved most valuable was a collection of cracked photos, note pages and varied memorabilia that had been stored in an old shoebox. From that random, somewhat dusty and faded selection, I was able to glean much of this forgotten woman's life. I felt I had created a most uplifting story; chronologically appropriate and as factual as I could possibly determine, so what should I do with it? I needed to know if it – everything about it, language, spelling, structure, all that – would be acceptable for publishing. Two earlier books for young readers – ages seven to 12 – which I had sent to a big-name publisher had been turned down, but since then I had been lucky in writing competitions and I'd had one short story read over the air; perhaps it was now worth trying again.

I remembered how in 2009, prolific author Ken Vincent had suggested I contact the Ginninderra Press publisher Stephen Matthews, when I wanted a speaker on the topic of publishing to speak to the Tea Tree Gully Library Writers' Group. I had been impressed when Stephen had refused a fee for his talk in which he emphasised that publishing was subject to certain standards and acceptance was not automatic. I asked his advice and subsequently packed up the manuscript and posted it off to Ginninderra Press (GP). Before long, I had an email from Brenda; they had given it a tick of approval. GP published *Paper Chase* in 2011, its title unequivocal in reflecting the story of its development. My memoir of Mary Ellen Kerr Peach was to become my first published book.

I gave copies to the younger women and girls in my family who were direct descendants of Mary Kerr Peach. Whoever in the ever-widening family read that little book would learn something of their heritage, her legacy. One teenager exclaimed, 'I have a Scottish suffragist teacher as an ancestor! Wow!' I knew then I had done the right thing by my once-forgotten grandmother. The broadcaster Peter Goers, on ABC 891, invited me to speak about it on air and was very complimentary. I took the book on some speaking engagements and it proved popular. Such wide acceptance was new to me and I was encouraged to revisit a number of my earlier works and check my notes as to feedback.

For some years preceding the memoir, I had enjoyed writing short stories. It had been a huge boost for my self-confidence when, back in 2005, one was accepted for reading over the air by Jenny Molnar on the Radio Adelaide programme. I had also written comedy stories and rhyming riddles for my grandchildren and was delighted when some were bought by the NSW *Education Magazine*. So I selected some of the earlier short stories and organised a quirky and slightly spooky compilation in 2013, totalling about 21,000 words. I submitted them to GP as a collection for appraisal, with 'quirkiness' as a theme. To my delight, Stephen accepted the stories – with some worthy recommendations.

I gave this second book the title *Jumping the Cracks*, dedicating the collection to 'all those who share my realisation that, walking as we do the ordinary path of everyday existence, we may sometimes fail to know that on either side of that path and under the cracks between, lies the unpredictable and the unexplained'. Fred, my husband, and I had great fun photographing the cover, using fishing line to suspend a pair of red shoes over a range of old paving stones. This book proved a success with various community groups. Peter Goers told me, when he was interviewing me about this one, that it reminded him of Saki. Praise indeed!

It was most encouraging that Peter knew of GP and complimented it – vicariously – on catering for aspiring writers and encouraging the craft of writing. As I write this, it is worth knowing that on the three occasions I have been on his programme he has commented favourably about GP's philosophy in enabling new writers to be published. I know I am not the only one of the GP writers to appreciate Stephen and Brenda's encouragement and judgement.

So, where to go after *Jumping the Cracks*? I indulged in more short story writing at the writing groups, enjoying the discipline of set topics. I submitted some stories to Kim Dodsworth, the Queensland storyteller on Radio 4RPH. He reasons 'the best short stories take only as long to read as a cappuccino takes to be enjoyed', so pruning words for him to read is a necessary art. By a marvellous coincidence, his requirement for a nine-minute broadcast at 1,500 words fits perfectly into my own mental scribing mechanics. Kim has broadcast 19 of mine so far. I later recorded some other stories myself and Brenda Matthews kindly gave me an appraisal of them. They have been popular sellers at gigs and I also donate them to groups and my ophthalmologist, to give to people with vision problems.

Then Stephen and Brenda suggested I have a go at writing poetry, in different styles. So I pulled out some previous poetic efforts I had written for competitions. I had won poetry competitions at the Salisbury Writers' Festival in 2008 and 2009, and at the 2011 Tea Tree Gully Poetry Festival in 2011. So when GP initiated an anthology, I was pleased to be asked to contribute poems or prose for *The Heart of Port Adelaide* in 2011 and *Collecting Writers*, published in 2013. These publications were beautifully produced by GP and made popular gifts. I think the anthologies spread the message of encouragement, when people can judge for themselves the variety of lovely, descriptive verse by other GP writers.

Writing as a craft is a mix of sheer enjoyment and pure selfishness. I found myself growing busier and realised I was planning my days around my writing, not my writing around my days. On a positive note, I was developing my techniques. I would contact Stephen and Brenda to sound out any new thoughts and always found Stephen to be quite analytical in his criticism (criticism in the proper sense) yet always positive in his encouragement. I know that I'm not alone in feeling that GP is almost one big family – a feeling strengthened when Fred and I with many others were invited to Stephen and Brenda's wedding in 2012; a heart-warming occasion that brightened a chilly August day.

This encouragement flowed when the Ginninderra Pocket series began in 2014; Pocket Poets first, then Pocket Polemics, Pocket Places and Pocket People. GP writers were invited to submit poetry or prose for these chapbooks. I didn't manage a Pocket Polemic but wrote a Pocket Poet, *Take Time*; for Pocket People, *Rupe*; and for Pocket Places, *Insulae*. I was delighted when *Take Time* was featured as the East Avenue Books' 2015 Poet for March. At this point I recognise with thanks not only Stephen and Brenda's encouragement but also their teamwork with Joan and Peter of East Avenue Books.

I had this feeling I should challenge myself and try writing a full-length novel. I didn't know if it could be realised but remembered my mother's adage of years ago: 'It's better to try and fail than fail to try.' I was restless. I liked history; my grandmother's tale had included her suffragist aspirations. Was that the way to go?

So – a subject? I read biographies and histories of Adelaide's early settlers, written by more accomplished writers than myself – Adelaide academics Helen Jones, Susan Magarey and Elizabeth Mansutti – and Catherine Helen Spence's diaries. Then, on visiting a school, I picked up a copy of a shiny school text entitled *Mary Lee – Let her name be honoured*, by Elizabeth Mansutti. I flicked through the pages and realised that Mary Lee was the woman whose energies and dedication were a primary influence in our gaining the vote. When I remarked on this, my young escort glanced over and shrugged her shoulders. 'Oh, her. We did her in Year 10.'

That remark stayed with me. I read and learned it was Mary Lee's persistent drive, energy, dedication and campaigning that persuaded Parliament to grant South Australian women the power to vote, to put governments in and governments out, and nominate for seats in Parliament. That was in 1894 and Mary's influence was acknowledged by Charles Kingston, premier at the time. And we were the first in the country. Yet that young student thought Mary Lee was just another fact in a history curriculum.

Could I lift Mary Lee from the classroom shelf so that people like me would know how some of the political and social benefits 21st century women enjoy are due to her – and a few of her contemporaries? Her achievements were well documented, but few personal papers were to be found. Could I research and write such a book? Elizabeth Mansutti in her book had resurrected Mary Lee; I wanted to put the flesh on her bones. But how?

Then opportunity struck – a mixed blessing for me. At the end of 2013 I was diagnosed with cancer. As the year turned, surgery and weeks of radiotherapy and recuperation followed. I needed a distraction, an alternative focus, to keep me grounded.

It is pertinent at this point to say how much I value my membership of two local writing groups. My fellow members, friends and colleagues gave me the support I needed – personally and professionally. One group particularly has a policy of offering positive criticism to members' writings and favours the short story. Another, an evening group, enjoys poetry also and has recently co-presented the Tea Tree Gully Poetry Festival and competition in cahoots with the Tea Tree Gully Library. Listening, learning and gaining feedback from the members has been, and is, invaluable. No matter how much we think we know, there is always more to learn.

I reopened my files on Mary Lee and buried myself in plotting, then drafting. I now had the time to plan plot and sequence. Mary's achievements were well documented, from Hansard to newspaper archives, yet no personal papers could be found. I read that she had been 'unladylike in her arguments for women'. Had she been an embarrassment to her family? Her fights for women's rights, recognition and her caring and concerns – such empathy – were well documented in her many letters to the editor of the papers of the day. Many of her letters debating a point advocated common sense. That word was my hook.

This woman's determination and her pugnacious support of disadvantaged girls and women intrigued me. I was determined to write the story I felt buzzing round my brain. I felt that to increase its appeal to 21st century women, I needed a foil to those classroom curriculum characteristics; perhaps another, younger woman who would benefit from the guidance and mentorship Mary Lee would have provided.

Beatrice Beauchamp came into being. I drafted a fictional plot that would tie in with Mary's true-to-life activities. Beatrice, recently married and with a husband serving in the militia, was pleased to make the acquaintance of Mary and her daughter Evelyn on the steamship *Orient*. When challenges lay ahead for Beatrice, Mary constantly stressed the commonsensical approach.

There were pitfalls, such as placing Beatrice in Barmera in 1880, when Barmera was actually still swamp land draining into a pond we now know as Lake Bonney. I had to rewrite references and change the geography of the book. That error caused a delay of about two months! And Brenda Matthews's meticulous editing recognised I had a woman's pregnancy lasting 11 months. I had to rewrite the sequence of events and relevant references. Stephen and Brenda's patience with my ineptitude (as I thought of it) was limitless.

I sloughed around in the despondencies – to cruelly paraphrase a cliché – a bit longer. This was my first ever full-length novel and it was going awry. I was bitterly disappointed at the Barmera error; I really crumbled under a crisis of confidence. It simply had not occurred to me that the township had not existed when Beatrice first went there but I should have checked. The challenges persisted. Linking Mary's actual calendar with the fictitious Beatrice, while still maintaining that fluidity, was at times like trying to solve a cryptic crossword. Paralleling fact with fiction and maintaining the flow of the story was certainly stimulating! To ensure an accurate depiction of Mary Lee I asked Elizabeth Mansutti, Mary Lee's biographer, and Elizabeth Ho, also a historian, if they would read through the penultimate draft of the book to verify my historical accounting. I scribed seven drafts altogether and Stephen and Brenda suffered three of those. Their patience was immeasurable!

I received the approval of the two Elizabeths for my depiction of the colony and of Mary Lee in my historical novel. I feared GP might not want to tackle it as it was almost 120,000 words. However, Stephen and Brenda persuaded me it was a good story. With Stephen's help and gentle pushing, the title eventually was settled as *Beatrice's Commonsensical Approach* – a catchy title. Its cover hinted at the romantic and I hoped its seeming levity, and frivolity, might attract the modern young women to our colonial history. It was published in April 2015.

I found buyers for some of the first copies and one young girl saw me in a supermarket and called to me, 'Mrs Mitson! I read your book. History really happened, didn't it?'

I was elated, no other word; I had brought history to life – for at least one person! I relaxed. Another reader emailed to say she loved Beatrice's story so much she 'couldn't put it down'.

I cleared my desk of the many months of paperwork stacked up from the 'commonsensical'. The Salisbury Writers' Festival writing competition was near its closing date. I wrote a poem, 'The Tiger's Eye', and submitted it; despite its being a rhyming story, it won a High Commendation. I hadn't thought it had a chance, being a rhyming story poem.

After the first print run of *The Commonsensical* (as I call it), I sent a copy to Peter Goers. I heard nothing for nearly five weeks. My fingers began to tingle and I dusted off my keyboard. I wondered if Peter Goers was reading my novel or if he'd consigned it to his WPB – he's a busy bloke. I sent him a copy of *Rupe*, hoping it might prompt some kind of response from him about my novel. It did, and he arranged for me to be interviewed on 29 September. In that evening show, he asked me how I could switch so easily from one style of writing – the 19th century colonial speech of Beatrice to the 1950s Aussie's language of *Rupe*. I decided to take that as a compliment. Importantly, he asked me so many questions about *Commonsensical*, his copy so full of stickers and pencil marks, I knew he had enjoyed it. He actually said so and asked if he could keep that copy. I was happy to say yes! After his show, I had a number of enquiries, which led to me writing some promotional letters to various schools and delivering two to librarians in girls' schools who wanted the book in their library. More young women to read of Mary Lee; I was delighted.

Yet despite my errors and their convoluted corrections, it seems the writing of a book, although mentally taxing at times, is physically easier than dealing with the end product. Promotion must follow the publishing; I found promotion not easy in Adelaide. In a cruel irony, we are so small in circulation terms that the mainstream outlets who could, and perhaps should, accept copies for sale will only do so direct with the publisher, and only certain publishers.

The book is very South Australian in its history and geography, and, with Mary Lee, in its social development. I know local people love to identify with places and events they recognise; I would love the wide world to recognise our history and social demography and geography. Yet will its parochial character inhibit interests interstate and overseas? I simply do not know.

Similarly, it is very difficult to have a book reviewed. I take solace in the fact the book is also on ebook sites and I have actually seen a favourable review of *Commonsensical* on the Amazon UK site, and the USA and Australian Kindle sites. Interestingly, I read that in the UK, despite the popularity of ebooks, there has been a resurgence in paper books. It is seen as a disadvantage apparently that Kindle readers cannot loan their books to other readers.

However, after a very happy and successful launch of *Commonsensical* at Tea Tree Gully Library, co-hosted by Symon Williamson and Elizabeth Mansutti, I felt willing to leave Mary and Beatrice to their own devices for a while. The launch was not only of the book, but of this writer – back into the wider world of deserving and patient friendships. I have mentioned the convivial interaction of writers' launches and musters. They are so important because they compel us to break from the very lone pursuit of writing and realise that to have friends, one needs to be a friend.

As a writer, dominated by thoughts, ideas, computer quirks and a keyboard, it is too easy to neglect friends, community and even family. When meeting other GP writers, particularly poets, it is so enjoyable to listen to their experiences and learn from them. There is such a variety of talent, skills and modi operandi to absorb, evaluate and take on board. Although my own preference is to meet over coffee and chat face to face, social media have one advantage: Facebook can be useful in promoting our work. It was through Facebook I was invited to speak about *Commonsensical* on *Words Out Loud* on PBAFM, a fortnightly programme broadcast out of Salisbury.

Stephen and Brenda are present at many of their writers' launches and these are such friendly and informative events. Some are held interstate, some nearby, as at friendly bookshops like East Avenue Books. I know from discussions with other writers that other GP writers appreciate, as I do, Stephen and Brenda's willingness to travel to these.

In 2016 Ginninderra Press celebrates 20 years of operations and since 2008 has been based in Port Adelaide. Time does not stand still for them. GP is a multifaceted enterprise with a single goal: I read once that Stephen Matthews's pleasure 'comes from propelling others into the spotlight and giving them the opportunity to achieve higher rewards'; a goal reinforced by the indigenous meaning of 'ginninderra' – 'throwing out little rays of light'. I know that I believe Stephen is deserving of public recognition for providing, at least over the last 20 years, the vehicle for amateurs to succeed, and the inestimable support that is his trademark.

As one of the writers who have benefitted from Ginninderra Press's philosophy, and philanthropy, I will share heartily in their celebrations and congratulate them warmly on their 20th anniversary.

Silk Road

Ann Nadge
South Australian poet and editor

As we respond to the challenges of changing technologies, the debate about paper or electronic books should be about how to preserve quality, negotiate freedom of speech and provide access in an ever changing world.

Jane Hirshfield in 'The Decision' (*Poetry*, May 2008) writes of the moment when inspiration turns an ordinary experience into a moment of insight, of transcendence for poet and in turn, reader and listener:

> As a sandy track-rut changes when called a Silk Road:
> it cannot be after turned back from

It can be argued that Stephen Matthews has turned the track rut of Australian poetry publishing into a silk road. Since 1996, Ginninderra Press (GP) has provided opportunities for new and emerging authors.

Sandy track ruts become silk roads when communities catch a vision of a promising journey or a rewarding destination. Stephen's vision has always included the fostering of communities of writers bringing new work to new audiences. What others may have seen as track ruts, Stephen saw as links between contemporary and historical contexts and their capacity to create important social records.

In October 1997, Stephen won a Canberra Critics Circle Award for Literature for his 'tireless contribution to the writing community' and in 2003, he received a Centenary Medal for his 'contribution to the writing community and ongoing support for local authors'.

In the same year, he compiled *How Did the Fire Know We Lived Here?* a best-selling collection of stories about the January 2003 Canberra bushfires which raised over $73,000 for the Bushfire Recovery Appeal. He also edited *Eye of the Soul*, a collection of interviews with writers for children and young adults.

Beyond his publishing business, Stephen Matthews has stimulated the growth of

Australian poetry, specifically by fostering communities of writers whose voices may otherwise not have been heard. Examples include publication of a book about the Hans and Nora Heysen legacies. *That Which My Eyes See* (edited by Ann Nadge) is a collection of work by South Australian poets with illustrations by artist Kevin Stead. Proceeds from sales of the book support work to maintain the historic Heysen estate, The Cedars at Hahndorf in SA.

The Heart of Port Adelaide project (edited by Brenda Eldridge) also enabled South Australian writers to reflect on the significance of the history of Port Adelaide as well as promoting interest in maintaining the character of the area. Similarly, *Collecting Writers* (also edited by Brenda Eldridge) shed light on the ways in which poets connect to the wider community through other creative pursuits.

Verbal Medicine, edited by Tim Metcalf, explores the relationships between medicine and writing as healing processes.

In this anniversary year, the anthology *First Refuge* (edited by Ann Nadge) reflects GP's commitment to social justice and to poets who are prepared to challenge silk roads and lead the public to a closer scrutiny of the many track ruts that often lie obscured by inattention or apathy.

Apart from capturing voices, technology is instrumental in changing track ruts to silk roads. GP has responded positively to contemporary challenges to the publishing industry. At one of GP's 10th anniversary events in Sydney in 2006, a panel was asked to comment on the future of books. The audience was left to ponder 'Are we fearful that books will disappear?' Even at that stage, before the extent of change became known, there was a prevailing sense of optimism. In the years since, Stephen has led with confidence by focusing on the idea that a book is what writers create and that technology is a mere carrier: beechwood, parchment, scrolls, wax tablet, clay tablet, slate, vellum, tablet, ebook! GP poets now have a choice of publication modes. After all, a book is what writers create and readers read.

In 2011 in *The Guardian*, Seamus Heaney wrote about the centenary of the Polish poet Czeslaw Milosz, who saw his home country invaded, witnessed the Nazi occupation of Warsaw, the destruction of the ghetto, the doomed uprising of the Poles against the Germans and the eventual seizure of power by the communists.

Czeslaw wrote of his duty as a writer,

> Whatever I hold in my hand, a stylus, reed, quill or a ballpoint,
> Wherever I may be, on the tiles of an atrium, in a cloister cell, in a hall before the portrait of a king,
> I attend to matters I have been charged with.

He won the Nobel Prize in 1980. Six years later, imagining the world after his own death, he wrote,

And yet the books will be there on the shelves, separate beings
That appeared once, still wet
As shining chestnuts under a tree in autumn,
And touched, coddled, began to live
In spite of fires on the horizon, castles blown up,
Tribes on the march, planets in motion…

Yet the books will be there on the shelves, well born
Derived from people, but also from radiance, heights.
And Yet The Books

As we respond to the challenges of changing technologies, the debate about paper or electronic books should be about how to preserve quality, negotiate freedom of speech and provide access in an ever changing world. There will always be track ruts and silk roads and Stephen has shown that by focusing on the critical bond between writer and reader, poetry books will continue to be well born.

Alive the Spirit

Barbara Olds
Canberra poet

The publication of Boundary Rider set me free – I no longer feared the past. In fact, I came to accept it as the vehicle that had brought me to writing.

It was 1998 and it was the community writing anthology *Alive the Spirit* that first brought Stephen Matthews and Ginninderra Press to my attention. The publishing house had been active for two years and was making a name for itself in Canberra.

The creative writing class I attended at the Belconnen Community Centre was producing an anthology and our tutor, Kate Deller-Evans, had been in touch with Ginninderra Press (GP) to have it published. As part of the editorial committee, I went with Kate to discuss the anthology with Stephen. It would be the first of many meetings I would have with Stephen over the following 18 years.

Out of the creative writing courses at the centre grew the Scribblers Writing Group. Beginning in 1999, Scribblers aimed to meet the need for course participants to continue their exploration of writing through a regular meeting of like-minded people. We set about creating a small writing hub in Belconnen. Through my relationship with GP, we were able to have published writers attend the group passing on their expertise to our members. We produced annual anthologies, which GP printed. Stephen even supported a writers' get-together at the Belconnen Theatre at the Community Centre where GP authors spoke about writing and gave readings from their books. The Scribblers/GP relationship continued throughout my management of the group.

From 1998 to 2005, the Belconnen Community Centre's Arts Program was very active. Included in those activities was the active pursuit of writers to submit works for various collections. *Park Voices* (1999) was the first of those collections. It presented not only the history of Margaret Timpson Park but the impressions and feelings that local residents and businesses had about the park. The launch of the book was held in Margaret Timpson Park in conjunction with the launch of several arts projects aimed at enlivening the park and encouraging local residents to use it. Two additional anthologies, *Ripples on the Water* and *Lifelines*, called for local poets and writers to submit work, again furthering the growth of community writing in Canberra. As with *Alive the Spirit* and *Park Voices*, I was given the opportunity to be involved with the editing of these collections, which entailed, of course, working again with Stephen Matthews and GP. I was learning what it was to be involved in the writing community.

In 1999 I started working for Ginninderra Press. I had run into Stephen at a writers' festival in Canberra and approached him about helping out at book launches. I was told that job was already taken but that he did need someone to represent GP to the local bookshops. Would I take that on? I said 'Yes.'

The challenge, however, was convincing local booksellers that supporting local writers would be good for business. I began with cold calls, dropping into bookstores unannounced and asking to speak to the manager. From there it became a four to six week ritual of sales calls, orders, deliveries and so on. After each round of sales calls, Stephen and I would meet and, over a glass of chilled white wine, discuss how we could increase the visibility of the press and further encourage local booksellers to stock the GP catalogue. Over the next five years, I became quite familiar with the GP writers, their books and the booksellers of Canberra.

If you want to see what's where in your town, go to book launches. The range of venues in which the GP book launches were held spanned a lot of the city. From small individual author launches at the Belconnen Library, Smith's Alternative Bookshop, Belconnen Community Centre, or Strathnairn Arts, to larger multi-author launches at Gorman House, Havelock House or the Dickson Community Centre, GP used them all. Although I hadn't started by working the sales table at the book launches, it wasn't long before I had taken over some of those duties. At those launches you could feel the excitement the authors felt as their books were introduced and, as they spoke themselves about their work, the sense of accomplishment was clear in their voices.

Voice, a journal of comment and review, was the collaboration of Stephen Matthews, Bill Tully and Ian McFarlane. In it, writers could express their thoughts on events, present book reviews or submit personal opinion pieces. Published by GP, it was my first opportunity to write opinion pieces about the things that were important to me – whether it was a rebuttal to a book review, my thoughts on being an American in Australia in the aftermath of 9/11, or my personal writing story. It also gave members of the Scribblers Writing Group the chance to write book reviews for the various editions. Public forums were held when the editions came out providing the opportunity for Canberrans to speak and question panel members brought together to discuss a specific subject. It was the type of grass-roots program I had not previously seen.

The year 2003 was a memorable one for Canberra. In January, fires swept down from the Brindabellas and devastated suburbs in Canberra's south. The physical and emotional toll the fires wrought affected all Canberrans. To provide a cathartic experience, Stephen Matthews called on Canberrans to submit stories of their experiences. *How Did the Fire Know We Lived Here?* was the result – community writing on a grand scale; writing for emotion, clarity and, perhaps, even acceptance; writing as a tool for healing. With proceeds going to the bushfire appeal, GP again showed its concern for the community and the importance the publishing house had in that community.

Personally, I had begun writing poetry when I was 13, but I had never gotten to a place where I identified as a 'poet'; that is, until I met Stephen Matthews. We often talked about writing when I returned each week from those sales calls. Over time, my confidence grew and I showed Stephen some of my work and he encouraged me to put a collection together. Admittedly, it took him a while to convince me, but I did just that. *Boundary Rider* was published in 2003. It was the book I had always wanted to write: poems which covered not only the angst of youth but the depths of the depressive illness that had overtaken me in my 20s. The publication of *Boundary Rider* set me free – I no longer feared the past. In fact, I came to accept it as the vehicle that had brought me to writing, but it would be years before I considered writing and publishing another collection of poetry.

I was surprised when Stephen asked me to speak at a forum about Fighting the Black Dog. It was an interesting panel comprised of other writers, academics and a psychiatric professional. For the first time, the confidence I had developed through my work with Stephen allowed me to discuss my writing and how it had developed through my illness. I was amazed when, after the presentation, members of the audience, complete strangers, congratulated me on my courage. It was a watershed moment for me.

During 2004 and 2005, my husband's retirement beckoned and I shed my involvements with GP sales and the running of the Scribblers Writing Group; but my relationship with GP continued. Even with GP's 2008 move to Adelaide, I kept in contact with Stephen, visiting him whenever we were in the area.

Stephen and Brenda came to Canberra in 2011 to launch Brenda's book *Facing Cancer* at Smith's Alternative Bookshop. At that launch I realised how much I missed the writing life and determined that I would put together another collection. It wasn't that I hadn't been writing poetry but, until that night, I didn't have the desire to again put myself on the line, letting others read my work and opening myself up to criticism.

That second collection was *Painted Souls* and it was published in 2013. While *Boundary Rider* was the book I *had* to write, *Painted Souls* was the one I *wanted* to write. At retirement, my husband and I began travelling more and more. It was on a trip to China in 2007, while watching a street cleaner using a besom (twig broom) to clean the footpath, I reflected on the dichotomy of the old and new in Beijing where all around old buildings were being torn down and modern ones constructed to take their place. Surely the souls there and everywhere were being painted by their experiences.

As for the future, I have plans for another collection of poems based, perhaps, on the concept of the maze, mandala or labyrinth. I have again taken over the role of convenor for the Scribblers Writing Group for which 2016 will be their 17th year. The opportunities to write are everywhere as long as you are willing to seek them out and as long as there are publishers such as GP to help writers achieve.

Throughout its 20 years, GP has evolved from producing staple-bound books with laminated covers, to plain thermal-bound books with paper jackets, to perfect-bound books and chapbooks, and now the option of print on demand. GP has used the technologies of the day to continue supporting the writing aspirations of Australians; bringing to readers a wide variety of thought, opinion and talent.

I have no doubt that the spirit of writing is alive and well at Ginninderra Press.

Finding the Light

Zenda Vecchio

South Australian novelist, short story writer and poet

I feel a compulsion to share my vision, the things I see and feel and imagine. I have to communicate it to the rest of the world.

The year is 2000. I am living in an old settlers' cottage in Birdwood with James and Matthew, the youngest of my six children (the others, quite a bit older, have one by one gone their separate ways). I have begun, after a difficult marriage break-up, to write again. (I had thought, when I got married, that if I gave up writing I would be like everyone else – normal. I was wrong. I ended up not being anyone at all.) Thinking of it, remembering, is like trekking backwards through a labyrinth. (If I go back far enough, will I find Theseus and Ariadne and the magic silver cord? Or will I simply find myself on my swing under the pepper tree chanting aloud words as I pump myself higher and higher?)

The year 2000 is a fitting place to begin, though, because it is the year that my novella *Mavis* was published by Stephen Matthews of Ginninderra Press; the beginning of a long relationship. I had by then had several stories published in various journals and magazines; the first, 'The Goat Kid', in *New Idea*, the second, 'Because of Rose', in the prestigious *Quadrant*. It was to me then, and even now, a kind of miracle because it meant I could do something. I wasn't quite a failure.

I began work on a young adult novel, *Listen for the Nightingale*, and it was in trying to find a publisher for it that, inadvertently, I stumbled on Ginninderra Press (GP). Like the shepherd at Ballarat who stumbled on a lump of gold.

Alice Shore and I had joined a writing group held initially at the Birdwood Community Centre (that in itself was an act of courage on my part, because it was before I had had anything published and I was very unsure of myself). Anyway, I don't know how, but Alice had discovered the SA Writers' Centre in Rundle Street. No one else in the group was very interested – for them, going to the group and reading their homework was enough. Alice and I wanted more. Were, you might say, driven. Again, I'm not sure why.

Except of course, a writer needs readers. Lots of them. And all different kinds. It may be true that I write for myself. But that's only part of it. I feel a compulsion to share my vision, the things I see and feel and imagine. I have to communicate it to the rest of the world. It's expressed best for me in the lines of the poem by Gerard Manley Hopkins, 'As Kingfishers catch fire':

> Each mortal thing does one thing and the same:
> Deals out that being indoor each one dwells;
> Selves – goes itself; *myself* it speaks and spells,
> Crying *What I do is me: for that I came.*

Anyway, Alice and I went up to the Writers' Centre and they had a lot of booklets there, writers' guides and so on, and I got one (actually the cheapest) – an A4 typed pamphlet, which they had compiled with all sorts of hints for would-be writers from how to write a covering letter to a list of appropriate commonwealth grants. More importantly, it included a short list of publishers. Among them was Stephen Matthews of GP, complete with a Canberra address and, most importantly, a telephone number.

I have a thing about phones. I find it very difficult to ring people especially if I don't know them. I get tongue-tied and find myself saying stupid things like 'How can I help you?' instead of the appropriate 'I wonder if you can help me.' But I made myself do it. After all, I knew fairy tales weren't true and no knight on a milk-white steed was going to come knocking at my door begging to publish my manuscript.

So I rang and Stephen answered. And I was immediately reassured. I liked the sound of his voice. I felt myself relax and blurted out that I had written a young adult novel and was looking for a publisher and the information I had told me he published children's and adolescent fiction.

Except he didn't. Short stories, poetry, biography, novellas…

'I've got one of those,' I said eagerly. 'It isn't typed or anything and I don't know how long it is but I think it's about 12,000 words. Would you be interested in looking at that?'

He said to send it. I put the phone down and my hands were trembling. I hadn't really thought about getting my story *Mavis* published. It was far too long for a short story; none of the places I sent my other stories to accepted stories longer than 5,000 words, neither did the various competitions. And I couldn't make *Mavis* shorter or longer. It stubbornly persisted in being the length it was.

So now I was faced with the challenge of putting it on the computer – a skill I was still painfully learning. Originally, my son James had typed my stories for me – at

$10 a story, he had found this a useful boost to his student allowance. His younger brother, Matthew, had offered to teach me how to do it for myself. (Later, I dedicated *Children at the Gate* to him in recognition of this.) So typing *Mavis* was, in itself, a memorable experience, just as slow as carefully copying by hand but so much easier. After all, backspace was there to eliminate errors or to make subtle changes. And an accurate word count! Pure magic. At the end of each session to be able to press a button and see how many words I'd actually written. A real sense of achievement that!

So off *Mavis* went. I was prepared for a long wait. Most of the editors I dealt with took several months to reply in my carefully stamped self-addressed envelope. (When I finally found a publisher for my novel, it was 18 months before they finally accepted it.) So when I got a letter – thick but not actually thick enough to be my actual manuscript – I could hardly believe it. An acceptance. And more. A contract. An actual contract. Still confused, I read and reread it. *Mavis* seemed an unlikely thing for anyone to want to publish.

My story *Mavis* isn't like anything else I have written before or since. I didn't even write it in my usual slow painstaking way. I usually have everything planned out from the first sentence to the last. I recite bits to myself as I go about my daily life – walking, doing dishes, gardening, knitting. This has been the pattern of my life – telling myself stories, a lot of which never get written. But *Mavis* was different. I had the idea – saw the child, her parents – picked up my pen and began writing. (A method a lot of writers use, I think.) Exciting in a way because you have no idea where you're going. But you don't have much control either.

My friend Edgar Castle (sadly no longer with us) wrote the blurb for the back of the book. It seems appropriate for me to quote it here:

> A change-of-life baby or a changeling? A magic mirror or a paranoid delusion? Dreams or realities? *Mavis* projects the forest-dark world of ancient folk-lore into modern middle class domesticity.

So there you are. Mavis's world is still very real to me, its landscape rather like an Arthur Rackham drawing. It has its own power. Reading it myself, I am never quite sure if Mavis is an ordinary little girl or, as her mother comes to believe, a fiend.

So I signed the contracts and sent them back. It would be published. That was that.

Except…

I got a brief note back from Stephen. (Stephen, then as now, has never been one to waste words.) Ideas for the cover? Launch? Launcher? He was coming over to SA in November. If I could have the launch organised for then… He gave me a choice of several dates. Well and good. I stared at this slip of paper in horror. I had never even been to a book launch. Worse, I had no idea where to hold it. My own tumbledown cottage was obviously unsuitable and, anyway, who on earth could I invite? And who could I get to launch it? I didn't know anyone important. In fact, most of the people I did know were hardly literary.

Ros Dickenson (another dear friend no longer with us) came to my rescue. An artist in her own right, she designed the cover, a poignant image of a little girl that, for me certainly, somehow portrays the ambivalent nature of Mavis that is at the very heart of my book. Then Ros went ahead and organised the launch at Grand Cru Winery, even finding me a launcher in the person of Leonie Holmes, a prominent Mt Pleasant citizen. All I had to do was turn up and actually meet Stephen. Which, Stephen being Stephen, wasn't frightening at all. And lots of people came – Ros and I invited everyone either of us knew. It was very gratifying. I felt like a proper writer. Queen for a day, perhaps, with my adoring public. (That might be an exaggeration.) One thing I didn't know then (but rectified at subsequent launches) was that it was customary for the author to read out a (hopefully) exciting excerpt as an enticement for the guests to actually buy a book.

As I have indicated, this launch was the first of many. An examination of the books I have had published by GP is a record not only of my journey as a writer but to some extent the history of GP itself, its evolution one might say.

Mavis (2000) and *A Conversation with Emily and Other Stories* (2001) were published in the original stapled format and, as such, were limited, I think, to 14,000 words. Then came *Children at the Gate* (2005) a new, slightly more substantial volume (23,000 words) thermally bound with not only a dust cover but a proper spine complete with author's name and book title. *Tiger! Tiger!* (2008) similarly bound and so on, but Stephen had now left the ACT and had become a resident of SA. *Tiger! Tiger!* was followed by *Light on Dark Water* (2011). These subsequent books are all volumes of short stories. I have a reputation for writing 'grim' stories but I defend myself here by claiming that what I write about is something the Germans call *weltschmerz*, the world's pain, and since we are all aware of it, no matter how hard we try to pretend otherwise, I make no apology for it.

My next book with GP was *Becoming Kirsty-Lee* (2012), a young adult novel about a 13-year-old girl coming to terms with her parents' divorce. With this, I took advantage of GP's partnership option, where I contributed to the cost of printing. It worked out very well for me. It meant that I could have my novel published in the form I wanted it. As an editor, Stephen is very kind. I felt, have always felt, with GP, that I was in control of my manuscript. This was not quite the case with my other YA novel, eventually published by Greater Glider. I mean no disrespect to them – I am grateful for the opportunity they gave me – but I had to do quite a bit of rewriting and so on, which for that book may not necessarily have been a bad thing. If I wrote it now, it would, I think, be different, better. Which is one of the problems of being a writer. Hindsight. That cringing feeling of reading something you once thought perfect and knowing you could have done it better.

As a writer, I have increasingly come to feel that the relationship between writer and publisher has to involve trust as well as respect. My characters are very real to me; they are vulnerable enough because of the situations they are in. (I was going to say the situations I have placed them in but it isn't quite like that.) I feel they are safe in Stephen's hands. That might sound ridiculous but it's how I feel. I have had a few bad experiences with editors of magazines changing things without asking my permission. Truly that feels like a violation. If they had asked (as Greater Glider did), we could have reached a compromise. I wouldn't have minded that. I consider myself reasonable even when it concerns my writing. Stephen has always respected my integrity as a writer and I in turn have respected his integrity as an editor. Obviously (well, to me anyhow) his grammar is better than mine. I am not convinced that it is 'veranda' not 'verandah' but that is of no real concern. As my granddaughter would say, 'Whatever!'

Because of the success of *Becoming Kirsty-Lee*, I put my adult novel *The Swan's Egg* into Stephen's hands as well. This was an act of faith. I think it is some 70,000 words and was the painful work of years. After a long delay (testimony to Stephen's patience), due to problems I had with the cover design, it was published in 2014.

The manuscript for my next collection of short stories, *Spindrift*, had already been accepted by Stephen when he emailed to tell me that his new publishing adventure (seems an appropriate word to me at any rate) was a print on demand format and this would mean I could fit many more stories into *Spindrift*. Wild excitement among my stories then, all demanding that now at last they could have their place in the sun!

Stephen then told me he was using this format to reprint all the previous stapled and thermal-bound books (if the author so desired of course). So that led to *Spotted Leaves*, which contains a selection of my stories from my four previous collections. I feel a sense of satisfaction at this, as if somehow my stories are saved for future generations.

But GP keeps evolving like some exotic underwater species. Because now there are Pocket Poets, chapbooks edited by Stephen's wife, Brenda Eldridge. They are like a flock of birds, all with bright distinctive plumages. (I think I might have mixed my metaphors, but no matter; I am after all a creative writer.) There are other Pockets – Polemics, People and Places, but I am not represented in them. Only the poets. Mine is called *Fractals* and it has been a great joy for me to hold it in my hands, because I always wanted to be a poet.

Then (at the launch of *Spindrift*, in fact) it was announced that GP had taken over Picaro Press and were going to do another series of chapbooks, again edited by Brenda. I emailed her and asked if I could be one of those too. The result is *Luminous*, perhaps more sophisticated (in appearance, not content), slightly longer and with interesting vellum pages as a sort of frontispiece and also just before the back cover.

Maybe it is a bit pretentious but all my books lined up are rather like GP on Parade.

So there you have it. My involvement over the years with Stephen Matthews and Ginninderra Press.

At my first launch, Leonie Holmes pointed out that 'ginninderra' was a word of Aboriginal origin meaning 'throwing out little rays of light'. I don't know if Stephen was aware of that when he chose it as the name for his publishing company but of course it is appropriate.

I am obsessed with light, a theme common to a lot of my work. Over the years, the light generated by GP has grown stronger. I, with the rest of the Ginninderra Press writers, reach towards it like young plants seeking the sun. Phototropism. It is a potent image. All of us flourishing in a light that might otherwise have been denied us. I can only say how much it has meant to me as a writer and an individual.

Awards & Commendations

2015
Uncle Adolf (Craig Cormick), Winner, Fiction, ACT Writing & Publishing Awards

2014
Meat Pies & Mumbling Blokes (Margitta Acker), Highly commended, Non-fiction, ACT Writing & Publishing Awards

Extravagance (Irene Wilkie), Highly commended, Poetry, ACT Writing & Publishing Awards

2013
The Blue Roses of Ororoo (Margaret Visciglio), Winner, People's Choice Award, SA Writers Festival

First… Then… (Melinda Smith), Winner, Poetry, ACT Writing & Publishing Awards

The Love Procession (Suzanne Edgar), Highly commended, Poetry, ACT Writing & Publishing Awards

The Cancellation of Clouds (P.S. Cottier), Second prize, Poetry, Society of Women Writers NSW Biennial Book Awards

Waiting for the Southerly (Susan McCreery), Commended, FAW Anne Elder Award for a first collection 2012

2012
Indigo Book of Australian Prose Poems (ed. Michael Byrne), Winner, Poetry, ACT Writing & Publishing Awards

Hard Cases, Brief Lives (Warwick Anderson), Shortlisted, Mary Gilmore Award 2010/11

2011
A Siege of Contraries (Helen Rose Mitchell), Winner, People's Choice Award, SA Writers Festival

A Man of Emails (Michael Byrne), Winner, Poetry, ACT Writing & Publishing Awards

A Quiet Day (P.S. Cottier), Highly commended, Society of Women Writers NSW Biennial Book Awards

The Rough End of the Stick (Ian Rae), Highly commended, Fiction, ACT Writing & Publishing Awards

2010
Hornet Bank (Gordon Reid), Winner, Fiction, ACT Writing & Publishing Awards

Before Afterwards (Leon Trainor), Winner, Poetry, ACT Writing & Publishing Awards

Of Cheese & Chutney (Ian McFarlane), Highly commended, Non-fiction, ACT Writing & Publishing Awards

Futures Trading (Craig Cormick), Runner-up, Fiction, ACT Writing & Publishing Awards

The Wardrobe (Moya Pacey), Runner-up, Poetry, ACT Writing & Publishing Awards

2009

Smoke & Mirrors (Kel Robertson), Joint winner, Fiction, Ned Kelly Awards; Winner, Fiction, ACT Writing & Publishing Awards

Sleeping Alone (Michael Thorley), Winner, Poetry, ACT Writing & Publishing Awards

The Glass Violin (P.S. Cottier), Highly commended, Society of Women Writers NSW Biennial Book Awards

Still Life, Other Life (Barbara Fisher), Highly commended, Society of Women Writers NSW Biennial Book Awards

Bird in the Egg (Steve Holden), Shortlisted, Arts Queensland Steele Rudd Australian Short Story Award

2008

Rainbow (Jennifer Horsfield), Winner, Non-fiction, ACT Writing & Publishing Awards

Not a Flotation Device (Peter Frankis), Winner, Fiction, ACT Writing & Publishing Awards

Sundance of Shadow (Kylie Oakes), Winner, Ron Euling Award for Writing

Chooks in the City (Alyson Hill), Commended, Non-fiction, ACT Writing & Publishing Awards

2007

Ghosts in the Helmet Trees (Rory Steele), Winner, Fiction, ACT Writing & Publishing Awards

Secrets (ed. Stephen Matthews), Winner, Children's, ACT Writing & Publishing Awards

Tangible Shadows (Dawn Bruce), Winner, Society of Women Writers NSW Biennial Book Awards

Famine in Newcastle (Ryan O'Neill), Shortlisted, Arts Queensland Steele Rudd Australian Short Story Award

And They're Still Falling (eds Olwyn Broder, Venie Holmgren & Anabel Macdonald), Highly commended, Non-fiction, ACT Writing & Publishing Awards

The Painted Lady (Suzanne Edgar), Highly commended, Poetry, ACT Writing & Publishing Awards

Blundstones & a Brown Dog (Christopher Nailer), Highly commended, Poetry, ACT Writing & Publishing Awards

Polishing the Silver (Jennifer Chrystie), Commended, FAW Anne Elder Award for a first collection

2006

A Funny Thing Happened at 27,000 Feet (Craig Cormick), Winner, Arts Queensland Steele Rudd Australian Short Story Award

Southbound (Michael Byrne), Winner, Poetry, ACT Writing & Publishing Awards

How To Succeed Without Really Winning (George Huitker), Winner, Memoir, ACT Writing & Publishing Awards

Frieda & the Cops (Elanna Herbert), Runner-up, Fiction, ACT Writing & Publishing Awards

Worlds Turned Upside Down (Rochelle Ball), Runner-up, Memoir, ACT Writing & Publishing Awards

It Can't Be Forever (Tamara Jermolajew), Runner-up, Memoir, ACT Writing & Publishing Awards

Torture (Peter Reddy), Runner-up, History, ACT Writing & Publishing Awards

Body Image Body Scrimmage, Yogie Award for Outstanding Achievement in Youth Participation

2005

Unfinished Journey (Michael Thwaites), Winner, Poetry, ACT Writing & Publishing Awards

Trouble in the Garden (Peter Frankis), Winner, Fiction, ACT Writing & Publishing Awards; Shortlisted, Arts Queensland Steele Rudd Australian Short Story Award

Mapless in Underland (Melinda Smith), Commended, Poetry, ACT Writing & Publishing Awards

2004

You (Narelle Wickham), Winner, Fiction, ACT Publishing Awards

Indigo Book of Modern Australian Sonnets (ed. Geoff Page), Winner, Poetry, ACT Publishing Awards

Kiandra Gold (Hugh Capel), Highly Commended, Fiction, ACT Publishing Awards

Cold Touch (Lawrence Bourke), Highly Commended, Poetry, ACT Publishing Awards

Into the No Zone (Tim Metcalf), Highly Commended, Poetry, ACT Publishing Awards

'How did the fire know we lived here?' (ed. Stephen Matthews), Highly Commended, Non-fiction, ACT Publishing Awards

Princess of Cups (Craig Cormick), Shortlisted, Arts Queensland Steele Rudd Australian Short Story Award

2003

Cut Lunch (Chris Andrews), Winner, FAW Anne Elder Award for a first collection

2001

Blue (Jennifer Compton), Shortlisted, NSW Premier's Literary Awards

2000

Collateral Damage (Geoff Page), Highly Commended, ACT Book of the Year

About the Contributors

Thérèse Corfiatis lives in Ulverstone, on Tasmania's beautiful north-west coast. She is married, with two sons. Therese began writing poems as a 10-year-old, drawing inspiration from her deep love of the natural world, and social justice issues. Ginninderra Press has published six collections of her poetry and two Pocket Poets.

Bill Cotter is a retired secondary school teacher, living with his wife, Kay, in Bairnsdale. His award-winning poems and stories have been published throughout Australia. He has conducted poetry writing workshops for adults and children. He has a teaching qualification in speech and drama and this has enabled him to teach voice production.

Brenda Eldridge has lived a full and rich life. She believes poets, songwriters and storytellers are the untarnished voices of history and the conscience of a community. Through her own writing and the words of the poetry she publishes through Ginninderra Press, Brenda wants to make people think.

Joan Fenney has been a journalist for nearly 35 years in both the electronic and print media. Joan's award-winning poems have been published in anthologies, newspapers and journals throughout Australia. Joan has published two poetry collections with Ginninderra Press and a Pocket Poet.

Ian McFarlane is a writer, critic and poet who happens to believe that literature and music still have largely unexplored roles to play in nourishing empathy, imagination and global sustainability.

Maureen Mitson is an occasional poet who feels fortunate to have won poetry competitions when her first preference is prose. Her short stories have been read over radio and she enjoys building credible fiction on careful historical research, as in the novel *Beatrice's Commonsensical Approach*, which is proving popular in girls' schools.

Ann Nadge has worked in all levels of the education sector as teacher, researcher, deputy principal, consultant, adjunct lecturer and lay chaplain. Ann's poetry is published by Ginninderra Press. She has contributed to several anthologies and edited two, including *First Refuge*. Ann is the poetry editor of *The Guardian*.

Barbara Olds lives in Canberra, having moved there 24 years ago from the USA. She has been writing since the age of 13. Despite a large backlog of work, her first collection *Boundary Rider* was not published until 2003, at the age of 54. Her second collection *Painted Souls* was published in 2014.

Zenda Vecchio is a South Australian writer whose short stories and poems have been published in a variety of journals and magazines. Several collections of these have been published by Ginninderra Press as well as two novels: one for adolescents, *Becoming Kirsty-Lee*; and one for adults, *The Swan's Egg*.

Acknowledgements

Rays of Light: Ginninderra Press – the first 20 years was based on 15 hours of face-to-face interviews with Stephen Matthews. The first interview was conducted in 2010 and formed the basis of the article 'A man of many words' that was published in *The Independent Weekly*, 23–29 April 2010. The subsequent two face-to-face interviews were conducted in November 2015, with follow-up questions in 2016. Also, information was gleaned from interviewing Brenda Eldridge in 2016. Background research and relevant information used in the book were gained from the vast number of articles about GP, GP authors and their books written in newspapers and journals throughout Australia.

I would like to thank Peter for proofreading my words and being an excellent sounding board while I worked on *Rays of Light*.

Thank you Chris Matthews for capturing the essence of *Rays of Light* in your brilliant photo and allowing it to be used on the cover of the book.

Thank you to the GP writers across Australia who contributed 30 words about their association with the press.

Thank you to Annette Jolly for your tireless archival work in collating the vast number of newspaper and journal articles written about GP during the past 20 years, and arranging them in such a logical and accessible manner. They have proved invaluable in researching GP's 20-year history.

A heartfelt thank you to Ian McFarlane, Barbara Olds, Thérèse Corfiatis, Zenda Vecchio, Ann Nadge, Bill Cotter, Maureen Mitson and Brenda Eldridge for so enthusiastically embracing the idea of contributing chapters about their writing history and important links with GP. Your chapters enrich *Rays of Light* and provide an insight into your writing lives.

Thank you, Brenda, for your warm hospitality and inviting me into your home so many times to help me gain an understanding of the vital role you play, and have played, in GP's history.

Finally, a huge thank you, Stephen, for entrusting me to tell the story of your beloved press and for allowing me to enter your world. This is not easy to do when you are a private person and the interviewer has a penchant for sometimes asking difficult questions! Stephen, you have shown the patience that you are renowned for in answering all my questions and responding to any subsequent queries I had in regard to the writing and compiling of *Rays of Light*.

Many GP authors have received significant awards for their writing or have been shortlisted (see pages 94–96 for the full list). However, all GP authors have seen their name in print and have helped to enrich the lives of readers in Australia and, indeed, throughout the world.

We hope Ginninderra Press writers will enjoy reading the history of the publishing house that they are a vital part of. We also hope people from all walks of life – whether they are readers, writers, or those who love to hear the story about a person pursuing their dream – will be inspired to read about Stephen Matthews and what one person can achieve through passion and determination.

Afterword

Stephen Matthews

It is a humbling, and in some ways startling, experience to see one's life through other people's eyes. In reading *Rays of Light* I have been gratified to be reminded of so many high points in the life of Ginninderra Press. On the other hand, I have also been saddened to realise that so many other high points and landmarks have had to be omitted. I wish every GP writer and every GP book could have been mentioned – they have all played an important part in the most fulfilling period of my life.

I must of course express my heartfelt gratitude to all those who have contributed to this insight into my 20 years of independent publishing. It is heartening to recognise that so many people have understood what Ginninderra Press has been about.

In particular, I must thank Annette Jolly, who eagerly took on the task of sifting through and cataloguing 20 years of press cuttings and retrieving so much that had been forgotten.

And Joan Fenney, who rose to the challenge of putting GP into the wider context of my life – I shall remain deeply in your debt.

Finally, I must express my boundless love for Brenda, who embraced not only me but also my quixotic creation – Ginninderra Press – and has helped me to ensure that our books continue to 'throw out little rays of light'.

www.ingramcontent.com/pod-product-compliance
Lightning Source LLC
Chambersburg PA
CBHW081418080526
44589CB00016B/2591